The KNOW Your BILL of RIGHTS Workbook

facebook.com/knowyourbor.com   knowyourbillofrights.com   twitter.com/knowyourbor.com

Copyright © 2011 by Oculus Publishers, Inc.

All rights reserved. No part of this book may be reproduced in any form or by any electronic or mechanical means, including information storage and retrieval systems, without permission in writing from the publisher, except by a reviewer who may quote brief passages in a review.

Published in the United States by Oculus Publishers, Inc.

www.oculuspublishers.com

For general information on our other products and services please contact our Customer Care Department at help@oculuspublishers.com.

Written by Sean Patrick

Designed by Andy Huff and Kiersten Lief

First Edition

Printed in the United States of America

ISBN: 9781466424562

★ ★ ★

DEDICATION

This workbook is dedicated to the brave, tough-minded patriots of the past and present who have sounded the alarm against the dangers of government oppression of the individual, and who have risked lives and fortunes to uphold their beliefs that government is but an instrument of the people, its powers forever subordinate to their rights as human beings.

★ ★ ★

What Makes This Workbook Unique?

"The beginning of wisdom is the definition of terms."

– Socrates

I have a fundamental problem with many constitutional books and texts available today: they simply *interpret* the Constitution for you. That is, they feed you other people's understandings and opinions of the wordings found in the Constitution instead of helping you understand it exactly as the Framers wrote it.

This is a dangerous approach as, like a never-ending game of Chinese whispers, errors accumulate as messages are relayed from person to person. And worse, violations of constitutional freedoms or restrictions, if not guarded against, can slowly become acceptable through common-law precedents.

I strongly believe that the integrity of the rights granted to us by the Bill of Rights relies completely on us not only being informed about this document and willing to uphold it but also fully understanding the literal and historical significance of each clause.

So, the question is, how can you gain a full and proper understanding of something like the Bill of Rights without having it explained and interpreted for you? Well, you start with the biggest, hidden barrier to understanding that almost everyone completely overlooks: *words*.

Simply put, if you have misunderstandings about the words used to communicate specific concepts, you will not duplicate the communication exactly—you will reach your own distorted interpretation. If I were to tell you that the children had to leave at crepuscule, you might wonder what I am talking about (unless you understand the word "crepuscule"). "Crepuscule" simply means the time of the day when the sun is just below the horizon, especially the period between sunset and dark. The sentence now makes sense, doesn't it?

In school, many of us were taught to simply guess at the meanings of words by looking at the surrounding context. This, of course, is a very unreliable method of study, as the person writing the text had a specific concept to communicate and chose the words based on specific understandings. If you want to receive the information in the same light, you must share the same understanding of the words used to convey it, not come to subjective understandings based on what you think the words might mean.

Author Philip Dick once wrote, "The basic tool for the manipulation of reality is the manipulation of words. If you can control the meaning of words, you can control the people who must use the words." This is especially relevant to constitutional matters. An insidious way to pervert the Constitution and Bill of Rights is to pervert or obscure, whether intentionally or otherwise, the meaning of the words the Framers carefully chose. Failing to comprehend the original meaning of these documents guarantees that the original message will be lost in translation and maybe one day even deemed outmoded and irrelevant in modern society.

This is actually a familiar concept in jurisprudence, aligning with the rule of construction, which holds that if a plain meaning of a law exists, it should be followed. As Justice Joseph Story said, "The first and fundamental rule in the interpretation of all instruments is, to construe them according to the sense of the terms, and intention of the parties." If a plain meaning does not exist, the reader must construe the language of the text so as not to contradict the document at any point, and the reader must seek meaning in its purposes or in the principles that it embodies as understood from "its nature and objects, its scope and design."

To preserve the original meaning and application of the Bill of Rights, this workbook will take a unique approach. It will not teach you my interpretation of the Bill of Rights or anyone else's for that matter. It will help you reach your own understanding by carefully defining key words, by having you study the amendments, by providing historical context and quotes from the Framers, and by challenging you with assignments that consult your understanding.

"Do not separate text from historical background," admonished James Madison. "If you do, you will have perverted and subverted the Constitution, which can only end in a distorted, bastardized form of illegitimate government."

As you will see, much emphasis in this workbook is put on the precise meaning of the words used throughout the bill, as a misunderstood word can lead to a misunderstood sentence, which can lead to a misunderstood paragraph, which can lead to a misunderstood page, and so on.

To aid in your study, a glossary has been included in the Appendix. It contains explanations of historical figures and events and definitions of words as they are used in this workbook. Further definitions can be found in a dictionary.

The definitions of words given in each drill, article, and the glossary are taken directly from one or more of the following dictionaries: *Oxford American Dictionary*; *Encarta World English Dictionary*; *Merriam-Webster Online Dictionary*; *American Heritage Dictionary of the English Language*; *Random House Unabridged Dictionary*; *Collins Cobuild Advanced Learner's English Dictionary*; *Cambridge International Dictionary of English*; *Webster's 1828 Dictionary*; *Webster's Revised Unabridged 1913 Edition*; *Columbia Encyclopedia, Sixth Edition*; and others.

It is going to take another person to do some of the actions called for within this workbook. Find someone who will help you. It can be your spouse, friend, son, daughter, parent, or anyone else.

You and your partner should work out spending a little bit of time on this workbook each day. Make a firm agreement to get it done together and stick to it.

As soon as you get your schedule worked out you should set up a quiet work-space that includes a dictionary you like, some paper, and some pencils. Once you have this all set up, you're ready to begin!

While the historical information shared in this workbook was culled from various sources and authors, my primary source was the late Leonard W. Levy, a distinguished historian, professor, and Pulitzer Prize–winning author. He deserves special recognition for his contributions to the field, and if you want to learn even more of the history of the Bill of Rights, I highly recommend Levy's *Origins of the Bill of Rights*, a principled, learned, and compelling treatise on the subject.

By the end of this workbook, you are going to understand your rights like never before and probably come to greatly admire the visionary, noble intentions of the Founders of this nation and their dream of a free society in which you have the right to express yourself, pursue your dreams, and achieve happiness.

Sean Patrick

Author, Know Your Bill of Rights Workbook

The Know Your Bill of Rights Workbook Study Guide

NAME: _____

DATE STARTED: _____ DATE COMPLETED: _____

PURPOSE OF THIS WORKBOOK:

The purpose of this workbook is to enlighten people on their Constitutional rights as they were intended by the Framers, and to empower and inspire people to educate others so that we can, together, stand up for these rights and preserve the foundations of liberty and of government by consent of the people.

HOW TO DO THIS WORKBOOK:

Study this workbook by following the steps of this Study Guide, which lists all of the reading materials and actions (drills, essays, etc.) you need to do. Read each article and do each drill and essay in the sequence given.

For your convenience, this workbook is laid out in the order in which it is to be done. Essay sheets are included.

IMPORTANT NOTE:

To aid in your study, a glossary has been included in the Appendix. It contains explanations of historical figures and events and definitions of words as they are used in this workbook. Further definitions can be found in a dictionary.

Introduction

READ: *Introduction* _____

Preamble

DRILL: Preamble Key Words Drill Part One _____

DRILL: Preamble Key Words Drill Part Two _____

READ: *The Bill of Rights Preamble* _____

ESSAY: Why do you think the Bill of Rights was created? _____

The First Amendment

DRILL: The First Amendment Key Words Drill _____

READ: *The Bill of Rights the First Amendment* _____

READ: *The Story Behind the First Amendment* _____

ESSAY: Give your understanding of the following statement:

"Congress shall make no law respecting an establishment of religion, or prohibiting the free exercise thereof…" _____

ESSAY: Give three specific examples of freedoms or rights this clause gives you and others. _____

ESSAY: Give three specific examples of restrictions this clause puts on the government. _____

ESSAY: Give three specific examples of ways the government could violate this clause. _____

ESSAY: Why do you think this clause is important in today's society? Do you agree with this clause? If not, explain. _____

ESSAY: Give your understanding of the following statement:

"…or abridging the freedom of speech, or of the press…" _____

ESSAY: Give three specific examples of freedoms or rights this clause gives you and others. _____

ESSAY: Give three specific examples of restrictions this clause puts on the government. _____

ESSAY: Give three specific examples of ways the government could violate this clause. _____

ESSAY: Why do you think this clause is important in today's society? Do you agree with this clause? If not, explain. _____

ESSAY: Give your understanding of the following statement:

"...or the right of the people peaceably to assemble..." _____

ESSAY: Give three specific examples of freedoms or rights this clause gives you and others. _____

ESSAY: Give three specific examples of restrictions this clause puts on the government or the people. _____

ESSAY: Give three specific examples of ways the government or the people could violate this clause. _____

ESSAY: Why do you think this clause is important in today's society? Do you agree with this clause? If not, explain. _____

ESSAY: Give your understanding of the following statement:

"...and to petition the Government for a redress of grievances." _____

ESSAY: Give three specific examples of freedoms or rights this clause gives you and others. _____

ESSAY: Give three specific examples of ways the government could violate this clause. _____

ESSAY: Why do you think this clause is important in today's society? Do you agree with this clause? If not, explain. _____

The Second Amendment

DRILL: The Second Amendment Key Words Drill _____

READ: *The Bill of Rights the Second Amendment* _____

READ: *The Story Behind the Second Amendment* _____

ESSAY: Give your understanding of the following statement:

"A well-regulated Militia, being necessary to the security of a free State…"

ESSAY: Why do you think the Framers felt a well-regulated militia is necessary to the security of a free state? Do you agree?

ESSAY: What type of attacks or dangers would a well-regulated militia protect against?

ESSAY: Give your understanding of the following statement:

"…the right of the people to keep and bear Arms, shall not be infringed."

ESSAY: Give three specific examples of freedoms or rights this clause gives you and others.

ESSAY: Give three specific examples of restrictions this clause puts on the government.

ESSAY: Give three specific examples of ways the government could violate this clause.

ESSAY: Why do you think this clause is important in today's society? Do you agree with this clause? If not, explain.

THE THIRD AMENDMENT

DRILL: The Third Amendment Key Words Drill

READ: *The Bill of Rights the Third Amendment*

ESSAY: Give your understanding of the following statement:

"No Soldier shall, in time of peace be quartered in any house, without the consent of the Owner…"

ESSAY: Give your understanding of the following statement:

"…nor in time of war, but in a manner to be prescribed by law."

ESSAY: Why do you think this clause is important in today's society? Do you agree with this clause? If not, explain.

The Fourth Amendment

DRILL: The Fourth Amendment Key Words Drill _____

READ: *The Bill of Rights the Fourth Amendment* _____

ESSAY: Give your understanding of the following statement:

"The right of the people to be secure in their persons, houses, papers, and effects, against unreasonable searches and seizures, shall not be violated…" _____

ESSAY: Give three specific examples of freedoms or rights this clause gives you and others. _____

ESSAY: Give three specific examples of restrictions this clause puts on the government. _____

ESSAY: Give three specific examples of ways the government could violate this clause. _____

ESSAY: Why do you think this clause is important in today's society? Do you agree with this clause? If not, explain. _____

ESSAY: Give your understanding of the following statement:

"…and no Warrants shall issue, but upon probable cause, supported by Oath or affirmation, and particularly describing the place to be searched, and the persons or things to be seized." _____

ESSAY: Give three specific examples of freedoms or rights this clause gives you and others. _____

ESSAY: Give three specific examples of restrictions this clause puts on the government or the people. _____

ESSAY: Give three specific examples of ways the government or the people could violate this clause. _____

ESSAY: Why do you think this clause is important in today's society? Do you agree with this clause? If not, explain. _____

The Fifth Amendment

DRILL: The Fifth Amendment Key Words Drill _____

READ: *The Bill of Rights the Fifth Amendment* _____

READ:	*The Story Behind the Fifth Amendment*	_____
ESSAY:	Give your understanding of the following statement:	
	"No person shall be held to answer for a capital, or otherwise infamous crime, unless on a presentment or indictment of a Grand Jury…"	_____
ESSAY:	Give three specific examples of freedoms or rights this clause gives you and others.	_____
ESSAY:	Give three specific examples of restrictions this clause puts on the government.	_____
ESSAY:	Give three specific examples of ways the government could violate this clause.	_____
ESSAY:	Why do you think this clause is important in today's society? Do you agree with this clause? If not, explain.	_____
ESSAY:	Give your understanding of the following statement:	
	"…except in cases arising in the land or naval forces, or in the Militia, when in actual service in time of War or public danger…"	_____
ESSAY:	Give your understanding of the following statement:	
	"…nor shall any person be subject for the same offence to be twice put in jeopardy of life or limb…"	_____
ESSAY:	Why do you think this clause is important in today's society? Do you agree with this clause? If not, explain.	_____
ESSAY:	Give your understanding of the following statement:	
	"…nor shall be compelled in any criminal case to be a witness against himself…"	_____
ESSAY:	Give three specific examples of freedoms or rights this clause gives you and others.	_____
ESSAY:	Give three specific examples of restrictions this clause puts on the government.	_____
ESSAY:	Give three specific examples of ways the government could violate this clause.	_____
ESSAY:	Why do you think this clause is important in today's society? Do you agree with this clause? If not, explain.	_____

ESSAY: Give your understanding of the following statement:

"…nor be deprived of life, liberty, or property, without due process of law…"

ESSAY: Give three specific examples of freedoms or rights this clause gives you and others.

ESSAY: Give three specific examples of restrictions this clause puts on the government.

ESSAY: Give three specific examples of ways the government could violate this clause.

ESSAY: Why do you think this clause is important in today's society? Do you agree with this clause? If not, explain.

ESSAY: Give your understanding of the following statement:

"…nor shall private property be taken for public use, without just compensation."

ESSAY: Give three specific examples of freedoms or rights this clause gives you and others.

ESSAY: Give three specific examples of restrictions this clause puts on the government.

ESSAY: Give three specific examples of ways the government could violate this clause.

ESSAY: Why do you think this clause is important in today's society? Do you agree with this clause? If not, explain.

The Sixth Amendment

DRILL: The Sixth Amendment Key Words Drill

READ: *The Bill of Rights the Sixth Amendment*

ESSAY: Give your understanding of the following statement:

"In all criminal prosecutions, the accused shall enjoy the right to a speedy and public trial, by an impartial jury of the State and district wherein the crime shall have been committed, which district shall have been previously ascertained by law…"

ESSAY:	Give three specific examples of freedoms or rights this clause gives you and others.	_____
ESSAY:	Give three specific examples of restrictions this clause puts on the government.	_____
ESSAY:	Give three specific examples of ways the government could violate this clause.	_____
ESSAY:	Why do you think this clause is important in today's society? Do you agree with this clause? If not, explain.	_____
ESSAY:	Give your understanding of the following statement:	

> "…and to be informed of the nature and cause of the accusation; to be confronted with the witnesses against him; to have compulsory process for obtaining witnesses in his favor, and to have the Assistance of Counsel for his defence."

ESSAY:	Give three specific examples of freedoms or rights this clause gives you and others.	_____
ESSAY:	Give three specific examples of restrictions this clause puts on the government.	_____
ESSAY:	Give three specific examples of ways the government could violate this clause.	_____
ESSAY:	Why do you think this clause is important in today's society? Do you agree with this clause? If not, explain.	_____

The Seventh Amendment

DRILL:	The Seventh Amendment Key Words Drill	_____
READ:	*The Bill of Rights the Seventh Amendment*	_____
ESSAY:	Give your understanding of the following statement:	

> "In Suits at common law, where the value in controversy shall exceed twenty dollars, the right of trial by jury shall be preserved…"

ESSAY:	Give three specific examples of freedoms or rights this clause gives you and others.	_____
ESSAY:	Give three specific examples of ways the government could violate this clause.	_____

ESSAY:	Why do you think this clause is important in today's society? Do you agree with this clause? If not, explain.	_____
ESSAY:	Give your understanding of the following statement: **"…and no fact tried by a jury, shall be otherwise re-examined in any Court of the United States, than according to the rules of the common law."**	_____

THE EIGHTH AMENDMENT

DRILL:	The Eighth Amendment Key Words Drill	_____
READ:	*The Bill of Rights the Eighth Amendment*	_____
READ:	*The Story Behind the Eighth Amendment*	_____
ESSAY:	Give your understanding of the following statement: **"Excessive bail shall not be required, nor excessive fines imposed, nor cruel and unusual punishments inflicted."**	_____
ESSAY:	Give three specific examples of freedoms or rights this amendment gives you and others.	_____
ESSAY:	Give three specific examples of restrictions this amendment puts on the government.	_____
ESSAY:	Give three specific examples of ways the government could violate this amendment.	_____
ESSAY:	Why do you think this amendment is important in today's society? Do you agree with this amendment? If not, explain.	_____

THE NINTH AMENDMENT

DRILL:	The Ninth Amendment Key Words Drill	_____
READ:	*The Bill of Rights the Ninth Amendment*	_____
READ:	*The Story Behind the Ninth Amendment*	_____
ESSAY:	Give your understanding of the following statement: **"The enumeration in the Constitution, of certain rights, shall not be construed to deny or disparage others retained by the people."**	_____

ESSAY:	Give three specific examples of freedoms or rights this amendment gives you and others.	_____
ESSAY:	Give three specific examples of ways the government could violate this amendment.	_____
ESSAY:	Why do you think this amendment is important in today's society? Do you agree with this amendment? If not, explain.	_____

THE TENTH AMENDMENT

DRILL:	The Tenth Amendment Key Words Drill	_____
READ:	*The Bill of Rights the Tenth Amendment*	_____
ESSAY:	Give your understanding of the following statement: **"The powers not delegated to the United States by the Constitution, nor prohibited by it to the States, are reserved to the States respectively, or to the people."**	_____
ESSAY:	How does this amendment give freedoms or rights to the people?	_____
ESSAY:	How does this amendment put restrictions on the government or the people?	_____
ESSAY:	How could the government violate this amendment?	_____
ESSAY:	Why do you think this amendment is important in today's society? Do you agree with this amendment? If not, explain.	_____

YOUR GREATEST DEFENSE

ESSAY:	What freedoms granted by the Bill of Rights mean the most to you? Which do you feel most strongly about or enjoy the most?	_____
ESSAY:	Why do you think it is necessary to protect such freedoms with laws?	_____
READ:	*Your Greatest Defense*	_____

★ ★ ★

INTRODUCTION

"In free governments, the rulers are the servants and the people their superiors and sovereigns."

– Benjamin Franklin

There is no record of history as bloody and battered as that of the power to rule. Countless millions have been marched to their graves during wars fought over the whims of and in the interests of lone individuals. Countless millions more have suffered lives of wretched, inescapable slavery simply because they were born to the wrong classes. Entire empires, built by the brilliance and diligence of generations, have crumbled in the hands of despotic kings with no more competence or intelligence than the lowliest beggar.

For many centuries, Man was locked in a social mechanism whereby an elite few arbitrarily wielded power, swinging the masses to and fro with little or no recognition or respect for the divine inspiration alight in us all. During Man's trudge through the dystopian Dark Ages, however, a radical idea emerged and, like a tale of Atlantis, fired imaginations to dream of a world never before known.

This simple concept was the first breath of what would become the greatest ideological transformation in history: all human beings, regardless of gender, status, wealth, and religion, are born equally free and with the right to the enjoyment of life, liberty, and property and the right to the pursuit of happiness. These natural rights are born with us, exist within us, and cannot be taken from us by any human power without taking our lives. Moreover, these rights formed fundamental law to which all man-made systems of domination or governance were subordinate.

This philosophy was a golden ray of light that punctured the gloom of past tyrannies, and it was the substance of groundbreaking recognitions of personal liberties such as the Magna Carta, the writ of habeas corpus, the Petition of Right, the Northwest Ordinance, and others.

As history would have it, the American colonists would be the people to carry this ideology to its full fruition. "America was opened," Emerson wrote, "after the feudal mischief was spent, and so the people made a good start. We began well. No inquisitions here, no kings, no nobles, no dominant church. Here heresy has lost its terrors."

Early on, American colonists embraced the philosophy that all men are by nature equally free and independent and have certain inherent rights that transcend human authorities. They also became accustomed to the idea that government only existed by the consent of the people, that the people created the government, and that the people have the right to change the government if it fails to serve admirably.

Aware of centuries of abuse by European monarchies and nobles, Americans also knew that without regular, fair procedures of law, there was no liberty. Fresh in their minds were the past horrors of vicious, arbitrary procedures that had been used to victimize religious and political minorities. History had proven that one's home could not be his castle or his property be his own, nor could his right to express his opinion or to worship his God be secure, if he could be searched, arrested, tried, and imprisoned in unpredictable ways, with no recourse. Corrupt authorities used bills of attainder to declare political undesirables guilty and sentence them to death without trial by jury. Ex post facto laws were notoriously unfair, for they made criminal any conduct that was not a crime in the past a punishable offense, retroactively increased the penalty for a crime, or changed the rules of evidence to obtain a conviction despite a past acquittal.

Visionaries such as Thomas Jefferson and James Madison saw that independence from Britain offered the American people a chance to reclaim rights regarded as supreme laws of nature and set up a government for themselves, created and limited by a supreme law that was paramount in all ways to it, yet unalterable by it.

Thus was born a new understanding of what a constitution was: cardinal law that would serve as the foundation of government, that would limit all branches of government, and that was unalterable by legislative authority. This differed greatly from the great English liberty documents, which limited only the crown but not the legislative power in any way (allowing Parliament to legalize any form of tyranny it pleased).

Madison made his intention of a new type of constitution clear at the Constitutional Convention, where he declared that the delegates had assembled to frame "a compact by which an authority was created paramount to the parties, and making laws for the government of them." James Wilson had earlier established his position that "all government ought to be instituted…to enable the individuals who compose [the commonwealth] to enjoy their natural rights."

The first draft of the U.S. Constitution was completed in 1787, but it lacked a vital component: a positive statement of inalienable rights guaranteed to all citizens of the nation. Jefferson stated this powerfully in a letter to John Adams, writing, "Let me add that a bill of rights is what the people are entitled to against every government on earth, general or particular, and what no just government should refuse, or rest on inference." Despite arguments that a Bill of Rights was unnecessary as the Constitution gave government no power to infringe on such rights, Jefferson worried that, without such a declaration, legislative tyranny would be an imminent danger for the decades and centuries to come and that executive tyranny would follow.

Introduction

After two years of controversy and debate, the triumph of individual liberty against government power, one of history's noblest themes, was finally epitomized in the American Bill of Rights—the inviolable laws to be added to the Constitution that guarded against abuse of "the great rights of mankind," as Madison put it.

As you will soon see, the Bill of Rights is a triumphant proclamation of sacred truths upon which freedom depends and a heroic defense of the individual against the majority, subject as it is to demagoguery and deception.

By the end of this workbook, you will not only fully understand and appreciate the liberties the Framers guaranteed you, your family, your friends, and society, but you will see how these liberties are the foundation of the lifestyle you currently enjoy. You will also glimpse the misery of life without them—a nightmare that our Founders dared to believe they could prevent from ever happening again.

Before we move on, however, I want to interject a solemn caveat. The Framers tended to be skeptical about the effectiveness of "parchment barriers" against "overbearing majorities," as Madison wrote. He had seen many violations of personal liberties in every state despite their supposed legal protections. So, you may wonder, how can a piece of paper come to your aid when it is needed most? The answer is, of course, that no scrap of parchment can float in and save the day. What good, you may wonder, is it for you—a mere individual—to understand and defend something like the Bill of Rights?

Well, just as we saw in the noble birth of this nation, enough people of the same mind and willingness to defy tyranny can overcome any opposition and secure their future. Richard Henry Lee and James Madison rightly observed that mere paper barriers might fail, but a Bill of Rights would serve as effective education of the people because it taught truths of freedom that must remain inviolate for there to be any freedom at all.

But what if the people were not given this education? What if they were ignorant of and indifferent to their natural rights? How would they guard against infringements or even know what constitutes a violation? They would not, and they would be, by definition, willing slaves. Who would guard their freedoms for them, though? Principled, admirable officials of government, you might correctly assume. But what happens when they are gone—who will replace them at the flagpole and keep it sturdy and true? With no resolute guardians to rise from successive generations, the flag will inevitably topple, and with it the greatest social evolution in mankind's history.

Jefferson stated this clearly: "Educate and inform the whole mass of the people.... They are the only sure reliance for the preservation of our liberty."

A cursory review of the chronicles of history shows that every civilization, empire, and nation has suffered or died from power accumulating in the wrong hands. Lord Acton famously wrote that "power tends to corrupt, and absolute power corrupts absolutely," and human nature, unfortunately, is just as predictable today as it was then.

"God grants liberty only to those who love it, and are always ready to guard and defend it," said Daniel Webster. The Founders were possessed of incredible compassion, insight, and forethought, but they are no longer here to protect us. Their legacy is not inscribed papers but a magnificent vision of a free, prosperous nation whose people, as Patrick Henry boldly declared, value liberty over all—even their lives. That vision must continue, and we are the only ones who can, individual by individual, give it light and strength.

True patriotism is belief in the ideals that this nation was founded upon; it is not ignorance of them and unthinking, endless devotion to government. So never forget the Founders' message that we the people are governed only by our consent, that we create government, and that we have the right to change government if it exceeds its limitations. Do not take your freedoms for granted lest they slowly erode until, like an ancient parchment, they crumble at the slightest provocation.

Become educated, encourage others to follow, and together, despite our divergent political leanings, we can stand united as human beings who recognize and respect each other's rights to enjoy life and liberty, to acquire and possess property, and to pursue and obtain happiness and safety.

Preamble Key Words Drill
Part One

Purpose of this drill:

The purpose of this drill is to ensure you understand the basic words you will be coming across while studying the Preamble of the Bill of Rights.

How this drill is done:

This drill is done with another person. Both people are to read the drill's questions and answers before starting the drill.

The person asking the questions is the "coach," and the person answering is the "student." The coach asks the student the question, and the student answers it. The answer does not have to be word-for-word; just the concept must be correct.

If the student gets a question incorrect, the coach shows him or her the answer. The coach then has the student explain the answer in his or her own words. Once the student has it in his or her own words, the coach re-asks the question. The coach then continues with the next question. Once they've gone through all the questions, they start again from the beginning.

How to pass this drill:

The student is done with the drill when he or she can answer all the questions correctly, from the first to the last, without missing any.

The point of this drill is not for you to just memorize the answers to the questions, it is to help you actually understand the information.

Note:

Words often have several meanings. The definitions used in this drill only give the meaning that the word has as it is used in this workbook. To get the full understanding of each word, look at its other definitions in a dictionary.

QUESTIONS:

1. **What is a *preamble*?**

   An introduction.

2. **What is a *draft*?**

   A first form of any writing, which may be changed.

3. **What is a *law*?**

   1. A system of rules that a particular country or community recognizes as regulating the actions of its members and may enforce by the use of penalties.

   2. A rule of conduct or procedure as a part of such a system, enforceable by an authority.

4. **What is *authority*?**

   1. Legal power or a right to command or to act.

   2. A person or group of persons that are given the power to command or control, especially to enforce the law.

5. **What is *legislature*?**

   A group of persons, usually elected, that has the authority to make, change and cancel laws.

6. **What is a *bill*?**

   A draft of a proposed law presented to a legislature, but not yet passed and made law.

7. **What does *legal* mean?**

   Provided or permitted by the law.

8. **What is *freedom*?**

   The ability to act, speak or think as one wants without resistance or restraint.

9. **What is a *right*?**

   A legal freedom to have or obtain something or to act in a certain way.

10. **What does *legislative* mean?**

    Involved in the writing and passing of laws.

11. **What does *independent* mean?**

    Free from the authority, control or rule of somebody or something else.

12. **What is a *misconstruction*?**

    An act of misunderstanding the meaning of.

    Example sentence: His misconstruction of my statement led to an upset.

13. **What is *abuse*?**

    Wrong or improper use.

14. **What does *declaratory* mean?**

    Stating and clarifying something, especially a legal right, status, order, or judgment.

    Example sentence: The declaratory note helped me better understand what was meant by the rule.

15. **What is an *end*?**

    The reason why something exists or why action is taken; the purpose or goal.

16. **What does *resolve* mean?**

    To make a decision by a formal vote.

    Example sentence: The new rules were resolved by the managers.

17. **What is a *body*?**

    A group of people united by their jobs or activities.

END OF DRILL

PREAMBLE
KEY WORDS DRILL
PART TWO

Purpose of this drill:

The purpose of this drill is to ensure you understand the basic words you will be coming across while studying the Preamble of the Bill of Rights.

How this drill is done:

This drill is done with another person. Both people are to read the drill's questions and answers before starting the drill.

The person asking the questions is the "coach," and the person answering is the "student." The coach asks the student the question, and the student answers it. The answer does not have to be word-for-word; just the concept must be correct.

If the student gets a question incorrect, the coach shows him or her the answer. The coach then has the student explain the answer in his or her own words. Once the student has it in his or her own words, the coach re-asks the question. The coach then continues with the next question. Once they've gone through all the questions, they start again from the beginning.

How to pass this drill:

The student is done with the drill when he or she can answer all the questions correctly, from the first to the last, without missing any.

The point of this drill is not for you to just memorize the answers to the questions, it is to help you actually understand the information.

Note:

Words often have several meanings. The definitions used in this drill only give the meaning that the word has as it is used in this workbook. To get the full understanding of each word, look at its other definitions in a dictionary.

QUESTIONS:

1. **What does *elect* mean?**

    To select by vote.

2. **What does *valid* mean?**

    Legally effective; having the force of law.

3. **What does *established* mean?**

    In place and generally recognized as being true or valid.

4. **What does *govern* mean?**

    To direct and control, either by established laws or individual judgments.

5. **What is a *principle*?**

    A fundamental idea or belief.

6. **What is a *constitution*?**

    A document that outlines the basic laws, rules, and principles by which a country or organization is governed.

7. **What does *arbitrary* mean?**

    1. Based on personal wishes, feelings, or perceptions, rather than on fixed rules.

    2. Based on the decision of a judge or court rather than in accordance with any rule or law.

8. **What is a *government*?**

    The group of persons who direct the actions of societies and states according to the established constitution and laws or by arbitrary decisions.

9. **What does *officially* mean?**

    With the authority of the government or some other organization.

10. **What does *formal* mean?**

    Done in a way that follows the established rules.

11. **What is a *state*?**

    A usually large group of people with their own government, not ruled by any other country; a nation.

12. **What is a *society*?**

    An organized group of people united either for a temporary or permanent purpose, with laws and traditions that control how they behave toward one another.

13. **What is a *clause*?**

    A part of a contract, agreement, will, or other writing.

14. **What is an *article*?**

    A clause or paragraph of a legal document or agreement, typically one outlining a single rule or law.

15. **What is an *Amendment*?**

    An article added to the U.S. Constitution.

16. **What does *ratify* mean?**

    To sign or give formal approval of (a treaty, contract, law, or agreement), making it officially valid.

17. **What is the *Senate*?**

    One of the two elected legislative bodies of the United States, composed of 100 members (2 from each state).

18. **What is the *House of Representatives*?**

    One of the two elected legislative bodies of the United States, composed of 435 members with 6 additional members who can't vote. Also known as the House.

    NOTE:

    The number of representatives for each state is determined by the population of the states (larger population means more representatives in the House). The 6 additional non-voting members are delegate chosen from each: Puerto Rico, The District of Columbia, and the territories of American Samoa, Guam, the Northern Mariana Islands, and the U.S. Virgin Islands. These delegates cannot vote, but can participate in debates.

19. **What is *Congress*?**

    The legislative body of the United States, composed of the Senate and the House of Representatives.

    NOTE:

    For a bill to be passed and made law, it must be approved by a majority vote in both the House and the Senate, and then must be approved by the President. If the President rejects a bill, the Senate and House can override him with a two-thirds vote in favor, and the bill becomes law.

    Additionally, the Senate and House have different exclusive powers. For example, only the Senate can approve treaties (agreements to international laws), while only the House can initiate spending bills and move to impeach people holding governmental positions.

END OF DRILL

The Bill of Rights Preamble

Congress of the United States begun and held at the City of New-York, on Wednesday the fourth of March, one thousand seven hundred and eighty nine.

THE Conventions of a number of the States, having at the time of their adopting the Constitution, expressed a desire, in order to prevent misconstruction or abuse of its powers, that further declaratory and restrictive clauses should be added: And as extending the ground of public confidence in the Government, will best ensure the beneficent ends of its institution.

RESOLVED by the Senate and House of Representatives of the United States of America, in Congress assembled, two thirds of both Houses concurring, that the following Articles be proposed to the Legislatures of the several States, as amendments to the Constitution of the United States, all, or any of which Articles, when ratified by three fourths of the said Legislatures, to be valid to all intents and purposes, as part of the said Constitution; viz.:

ARTICLES in addition to, and Amendment of the Constitution of the United States of America, proposed by Congress, and ratified by the Legislatures of the several States, pursuant to the fifth Article of the original Constitution.

Know Your Bill of Rights Essay

Why do you think the Bill of Rights was created?

The First Amendment Key Words Drill

Purpose of this drill:

The purpose of this drill is to ensure you understand the basic words you will be coming across while studying the First Amendment of the Bill of Rights.

How this drill is done:

This drill is done with another person. Both people are to read the drill's questions and answers before starting the drill.

The person asking the questions is the "coach," and the person answering is the "student." The coach asks the student the question, and the student answers it. The answer does not have to be word-for-word; just the concept must be correct.

If the student gets a question incorrect, the coach shows him or her the answer. The coach then has the student explain the answer in his or her own words. Once the student has it in his or her own words, the coach re-asks the question. The coach then continues with the next question. Once they've gone through all the questions, they start again from the beginning.

How to pass this drill:

The student is done with the drill when he or she can answer all the questions correctly, from the first to the last, without missing any.

The point of this drill is not for you to just memorize the answers to the questions, it is to help you actually understand the information.

Note:

Words often have several meanings. The definitions used in this drill only give the meaning that the word has as it is used in this workbook. To get the full understanding of each word, look at its other definitions in a dictionary.

QUESTIONS:

1. **What is an *establishment*?**

   The recognition of a church by law as the official church of a nation or state and supported by civil authority.

2. **What is a *religion*?**

   A set of beliefs concerning the cause, nature, and purpose of the universe, especially when considered as the creation of a superhuman entity or entities, usually involving systems of procedures and actions and often containing agreements as to what is right and wrong conduct.

3. **What does *exercise* mean?**

   To put something into action or use.

4. **What does *abridge* mean?**

   To reduce or lessen in duration, extent or range, authority, etc.; to diminish.

5. **What is *speech*?**

   Any declaration of thoughts, whether by words or other means.

6. **What is *censorship*?**

   The suppression of all or a part of something considered offensive or unacceptable.

7. **What is *freedom of the press*?**

   The right to publish and distribute broadly information, thoughts and opinions without restraint or censorship.

8. **What does *petition* mean?**

   To ask some favor, right, or other benefit from a person or group of persons in authority or power by submitting a formal, written request, often containing the names of people making the request.

9. **What does *redress* mean?**

   The setting right of what is wrong, often by giving something considered equal to the loss, injury, suffering, lack, etc.

   Example sentence: The redress of the wrongful punishment included a monetary payment.

10. What is a *grievance*?

A wrong considered as a valid reason for complaint, or something believed to cause pain, worry, sorrow, etc.

END OF DRILL

★ ★ ★

THE BILL OF RIGHTS
THE FIRST AMENDMENT

Congress shall make no law respecting an establishment of religion, or prohibiting the free exercise thereof; or abridging the freedom of speech, or of the press; or the right of the people peaceably to assemble, and to petition the Government for a redress of grievances.

★ ★ ★

THE STORY BEHIND THE FIRST AMENDMENT

"Without Freedom of Thought, there can be no such thing as Wisdom; and no such thing as public Liberty, without Freedom of Speech."

– Benjamin Franklin

THE ESTABLISHMENT CLAUSE

There has been much debate as to how one should interpret the establishment clause of the First Amendment. Does it dictate a separation of church and state, or does it merely prevent the establishment of a national religion? Does it allow government aid to religion? Let's look at the history behind this clause to gain insight into it.

Establishments of religion summon historical memories of religious persecution. In times past, an establishment of religion was a legal union between a state and a particular church that benefited from many privileges not granted to other churches or to those who did not participate in a church or did not believe in the accepted faith. Establishments of religion in certain American colonies before the Revolution meant compulsory attendance to religious services, public teaching of only the approved church's creed, marriage only legally performable by its clergy, stipends from public taxes paid only to its clergymen, and other various civil disabilities such as exclusion from universities and disqualification for civil, military, or religious office.

After the Revolution, exclusive establishments of religion in place from the colonial period crumbled. States that never had establishments renewed their protections against them. Other states ruled that religion was to rely on private, voluntary support. Nowhere in America after 1776 did an establishment of religion restrict itself to a single church or system of public assistance of one denomination alone. Only six states continued to provide public support to religion, and they were careful to ensure their establishments included many sects. Other states, such as Maryland, North Carolina, Virginia, and Georgia, banned public taxing and support for religion, making it purely private and voluntary.

With the First Amendment, the Framers intended to prevent religious inequality and restrictions of the free exercise of religious conscience, and that rightly included a prohibition of government establishing a national religion. James Madison stated that the "great object" of the Bill of Rights was to "limit and qualify the powers of Government" to prevent legislation in such prohibited areas as religion. "There is no shadow of right in the general government to intermeddle with religion," he wrote. He even opposed the inclusion of ministers in a list of occupations to be covered in the first census bill. He said that "the general government is proscribed from interfering, in any manner whatever in matters respecting religion; and it may be thought to do so in ascertaining who, and who are not ministers of the gospel."

When Madison introduced his amendments, the clauses on religion explained that no one's liberties should be abridged "on account of religious belief or worship, nor shall any national religion be established, nor shall the full and equal rights of conscience be in any manner, or on any pretext, infringed."

New Hampshire, the ninth state to ratify the Constitution, proposed a concise, clear wording of the matter: "Congress shall make no laws touching Religion, or to infringe the rights of Conscience." Virginia, New York, North Carolina, and Rhode Island also recommended an amendment on the subject. Virginia stated that "no particular religious sect or society ought to be favored or established, by law, in preference to others," and North Carolina and Rhode Island copied this verbatim while New York expressed the same idea.

In no way did the language of such proposed amendments imply that Congress should have the power to favor religion so long as no one group or denomination was preferred to others. Patrick Henry and his followers, who were responsible for the language of the amendment, were firmly against augmenting the powers of Congress; they were against the federal government having any authority over religious matters. In keeping with this belief, Virginia had defeated a proposal in 1784 that would have imposed a state tax on the people for the benefit of religion, distributing each person's money to the Christian church of his choice—a fight Madison led not because it referred too narrowly to Christianity, but because he opposed any kind of establishment of religion, whether for Christianity, Hinduism, Islam, Judaism, or any other.

In a letter to the Danbury Baptist Association in 1802, Jefferson wrote, "I contemplate with sovereign reverence that act of the whole American people which declared that their legislature should 'make no law respecting an establishment of religion, or prohibiting the free exercise thereof,' thus building a wall of separation between Church & State." Madison shared Jefferson's beliefs on the matter. Madison spoke of a "perfect separation" and believed that "religion and Government will exist in greater purity, without…the aid of Government."

Madison's own wording of the amendment he proposed to the House read like this: "No religion shall be established by law, nor shall the equal rights of conscience be infringed." The House debated the recommendation and there was disagreement about how to best word it so it would satisfy the popular demands for the forbiddance of an establishment of religion and guarantee of religious liberty. Samuel Livermore recommended that "Congress shall make no laws touching religion, or infringing the rights of conscience." When this was proposed to the

House, Fisher Ames motioned for it to read "Congress shall make no law establishing religion, or to prevent the free exercise thereof, or to infringe the rights of conscience." Livermore's wording was accepted and proposed to the Senate.

Six days later, the Senate substituted for the House version one that read "Congress shall make no law establishing articles of faith or a mode of worship, or prohibiting the free exercise of religion." The House refused to accept this version, and a resolution required a joint committee of three members from each branch, including four influential Framers (Madison, Roger Sherman, Oliver Ellsworth, and William Paterson). These legislators drafted the clause we now know as the First Amendment, and both the House and Senate adopted it and recommended it to the states for ratification.

FREEDOM OF THE PRESS

Sir William Blackstone wrote that the liberty of the press "is indeed essential to the nature of a free state." Madison described freedom of the press as one of the "choicest" of the "great rights of mankind." But how far should such freedom reach? Is all speech covered by free speech? Did the Framers intend that speakers should be free to incite violence directly against the government? Did they believe that knowingly spreading false, malicious, and damaging statements against others or the government is protected conduct? If the Framers did not intend for all speech, without exception, to be legally acceptable, what demarks the line of speech that is constitutionally protected and speech that is not? Let's look to history for the answers.

Nearly two months after the Constitutional Convention began, Charles Pinckney of South Carolina proposed various rights for inclusion that would form a partial bill of rights. One of them stated that the liberty of the press should be "inviolably preserved." The Convention adopted two of his propositions but passed over the rest, including one guaranteeing liberty of the press. On September 12, 1787, as the Constitutional Convention was coming to a close, a motion to include a bill of rights was defeated. A couple days later, Pinckney again proposed a free press clause. Roger Sherman reasoned that it was unnecessary as "the power of Congress does not extend to the Press." Three days later, the Convention adjourned, and so began misgivings about a Constitution that guaranteed some rights but omitted most.

Throughout the emerging nation, freedom of the press became a topic of heated debate, and there was a growing demand for its constitutional protection, but there was not yet a consensus as to what it meant, what its scope should be, and whether any circumstances would justify restrictions.

The prevailing thought among legislatures and judiciaries at the time was reflected in state constitutions and common law. Many state constitutions protected liberty of the press, but the understanding was that the government was only to place no prior restraints upon it: people could publish anything they pleased, but they might be criminally convicted for defaming the government. Such convictions established the common law. Chief Justice Thomas McKean felt this was an accurate and appropriate application of Blackstone's declaration that publishing "bad sentiments destructive of the needs of society is the crime which society corrects."

In a 1789 essay, Ben Franklin called for the use of cudgels to break the heads of those who would use the press for libel. William Livingston had declared in an essay that anyone who published "any Thing injurious to his Country" should be convicted for "high Treason against the State." Sherman framed a bill of rights in 1789 that protected one's right to express his sentiments "with decency," a phrasing that was understood at the time to exclude libels—personal, obscene, blasphemous, or seditious. James Wilson supported truth as a defense but otherwise agreed. Madison, in the times preceding the ratification of the Bill of Rights, never hinted at dissent from these views. Jefferson's 1783 draft of Virginia's constitution proposed that the press "shall be subject to no other restraint than liableness to legal prosecution for false facts printed and published." Jefferson singled out "false facts" or "falsehoods" for prosecution, but he implicitly opposed the prosecution of accurate information.

Simply put, many states upheld laws that stated freedom of the press was compatible with the prosecution for seditious libel and that even truth was not a valid defense. While no censorship would be placed on the citizens, every person was responsible if he attacked the government in speech or writing, and such actions would lead to a criminal prosecution in a federal court.

If criminal prosecution of verbal attacks on government seems to contradict the spirit of government by consent of the people, you are absolutely correct. However, the prosecution of seditious libel had its roots in centuries of English common law and, as this law was the basis of colonial law, it was entrenched tradition almost everyone in the colonies, including the Framers, instinctively accepted.

Fate, however, would not have it remain so. In the years following the ratification of the Bill of Rights, prosecutions for criticism of the government were infrequent, despite a habitually slanderous press. The federal and state governments refrained from prosecution in many instances because they realized such actions could backfire or fail because critics represented powerful factions and often prominent men. Moreover, people tended to distrust a government that imprisons its critics and protects from criticism its officials who, in many cases, had probably deserved it.

In 1798, the infamous Sedition Act was passed. It broadened the common-law understanding of freedom of the press and required that criminal intent be shown, it gave the jury the power to decide whether the accused's statement was in fact libelous, and it admitted truth as a defense. This was a great victory for those urging reform, but glimmerings of an even broader, more libertarian theory were already emerging.

The threshold of public tolerance had widened, and the freedom of the press was expanding to include the right to censure the government, its officials, and its policies and to publicize opinions on matters of public concern.

A new rationale for the meaning of freedom of speech and the press was expressed in treatises written by George Hay, James Madison, Albert Gallatin, Tunis Wortman, John Thomson, and St. George Tucker. These libertarians rejected Blackstone and common law, contemptuously denouncing the idea of no prior restraints but consequent punishment. Recognizing the obvious fact that a law inflicting penalties would have the same effect as a prior restraint, Madison wrote, "It would seem a mockery to say that no laws shall be passed preventing publications from being made, but that laws might be passed for punishing them in case they should be made."

Hay charged that the Sedition Act "appears to be directed against falsehood and malice only; in fact…there are many truths, important to society, which are not susceptible of that full, direct, and positive evidence, which alone can be exhibited before a court and a jury." Gallatin argued that if a citizen were prosecuted for his opinion that the Sedition Act was unconstitutional, would not a jury composed of friends of the government find his criticism "ungrounded, false and scandalous, and its publication malicious? And by what kind of argument or evidence, in the present temper of parties, could the accused convince them that his opinions were true?" These new libertarians maintained that the truth of opinions could not be proved, and thus, allowing "truth" as a defense of freedom, Thomson declared, made as much sense as allowing a jury to decide on "the most palatable food, agreeable drink, or beautiful color."

The rejection of conventional ideas struck at the heart of the matter when Wortman challenged the concept of such a thing as criminal seditious libel. Wortman concluded that such a crime could "never be reconciled to the genius and constitution of a Representative Commonwealth," advocating a truly radical position of absolute freedom of political expression based upon the belief that a free government cannot be criminally attacked by the opinions of its citizens.

Hay asserted that a citizen should have a right to "say everything which his passions suggest; he may employ all his time, and all his talents, if he is wicked enough, to do so, in speaking against the government matters that are false, scandalous and malicious," and despite this, he should be "safe within the sanctuary of the press" even if he "condemns the principle of republican institutions… censures the measures of our government, and every department and officer thereof, and ascribes the measures of the former, however salutary, and conduct of the latter, however upright, to the basest motives; even if he ascribes to them measures and acts, which never had existence; thus violating at once, every principle of decency and truth."

This novel and democratic theory was much more fitting to a society that looked at government as the servant of the people, existing only by their consent and for their benefit, constitutionally limited, responsible, and elective. Such a government, Thomson wrote, cannot tell a citizen, "You shall not think this or that upon certain subjects; or if you do, it is at your peril." The crime of seditious libel implies that the people are inferior to the state, and that their criticisms are unacceptable to their master.

An electoral process would be a charade if voters did not have the help of the press in uncovering and publishing past performance records and qualifications. An indispensable element of the press's societal role was that of a tribune of the people, sitting in judgment on the conduct of public officials; an essential function in the intricate system of checks and balances that exposed mismanagement and corruption and kept those in power accountable and manageable.

The press was also intended to be a safeguard of personal liberties. The Massachusetts constitution asserted that a free press was "essential to the security of freedom in a state" because the existence of various rights and freedoms depended at least in part on the alertness of the press to injustice, inequalities, and infringements.

These noble principles set a high standard of personal freedom and inextricably wove true freedom of the press into the matrix of a free and responsible government and the protection of liberties.

Know Your Bill of Rights Essay

Give your understanding of the following statement:

"Congress shall make no law respecting an establishment of religion, or prohibiting the free exercise thereof…"

Know Your Bill of Rights Essay

Give three specific examples of freedoms or rights this clause gives you and others.

Know Your Bill of Rights

Essay

Give three specific examples of restrictions this clause puts on the government.

Know Your Bill of Rights

Essay

Give three specific examples of ways the government could violate this clause.

Know Your Bill of Rights

Essay

Why do you think this clause is important in today's society? Do you agree with this clause? If not, explain.

Know Your Bill of Rights Essay

Give your understanding of the following statement:

"...or abridging the freedom of speech, or of the press..."

Know Your Bill of Rights

Essay

Give three specific examples of freedoms or rights this clause gives you and others.

Know Your Bill of Rights

Essay

Give three specific examples of restrictions this clause puts on the government.

Know Your Bill of Rights Essay

Give three specific examples of ways the government could violate this clause.

Know Your Bill of Rights

Essay

Why do you think this clause is important in today's society? Do you agree with this clause? If not, explain.

Know Your Bill of Rights Essay

Give your understanding of the following statement:

"…or the right of the people peaceably to assemble…"

Know Your Bill of Rights

Essay

Give three specific examples of freedoms or rights this clause gives you and others.

Know Your Bill of Rights Essay

Give three specific examples of restrictions this clause puts on the government or the people.

Know Your Bill of Rights

Essay

Give three specific examples of ways the government or the people could violate this clause.

Know Your Bill of Rights

Essay

Why do you think this clause is important in today's society? Do you agree with this clause? If not, explain.

Know Your Bill of Rights Essay

Give your understanding of the following statement:

"...and to petition the Government for a redress of grievances."

Know Your Bill of Rights

Essay

Give three specific examples of freedoms or rights this clause gives you and others.

Know Your Bill of Rights Essay

Give three specific examples of ways the government could violate this clause.

Know Your Bill of Rights

Essay

Why do you think this clause is important in today's society? Do you agree with this clause? If not, explain.

The Second Amendment Key Words Drill

Purpose of this drill:

The purpose of this drill is to ensure you understand the basic words you will be coming across while studying the Second Amendment of the Bill of Rights.

How this drill is done:

This drill is done with another person. Both people are to read the drill's questions and answers before starting the drill.

The person asking the questions is the "coach," and the person answering is the "student." The coach asks the student the question, and the student answers it. The answer does not have to be word-for-word; just the concept must be correct.

If the student gets a question incorrect, the coach shows him or her the answer. The coach then has the student explain the answer in his or her own words. Once the student has it in his or her own words, the coach re-asks the question. The coach then continues with the next question. Once they've gone through all the questions, they start again from the beginning.

How to pass this drill:

The student is done with the drill when he or she can answer all the questions correctly, from the first to the last, without missing any.

The point of this drill is not for you to just memorize the answers to the questions, it is to help you actually understand the information.

Note:

Words often have several meanings. The definitions used in this drill only give the meaning that the word has as it is used in this workbook. To get the full understanding of each word, look at its other definitions in a dictionary.

QUESTIONS:

1. **What is a *militia*?**

    An army composed of ordinary citizens rather than professional soldiers.

    NOTE:

    A militia can be called up by the government to serve full-time during emergencies.

2. **What is *security*?**

    Protection from attack or safety from danger of any kind.

3. **What does *bear* mean?**

    To carry something; to move something from place to place.

4. **What are *arms*?**

    Weapons of offense, or armor for defense and protection of the body.

5. **What does *infringe* mean?**

    To limit or reduce someone's legal rights or freedom, whether by intervention or not fulfilling some duty.

END OF DRILL

★ ★ ★

THE BILL OF RIGHTS
THE SECOND AMENDMENT

A well-regulated militia, being necessary to the security of a free State, the right of the people to keep and bear arms, shall not be infringed.

★ ★ ★

The Story Behind The Second Amendment

"Americans have the right and advantage of being armed—unlike the citizens of other countries whose governments are afraid to trust the people with arms."

– James Madison

We have all heard that an armed population is a shield against tyranny. Despite the fact that the Constitution does not authorize militias to wage war against the government—an act of treason—Americans theoretically have a right to insurrection to correct intolerable and systematic abuses. As endorsed by some state constitutions, Americans have unsurprisingly embraced the belief that a right of revolution is a natural right.

But does the Second Amendment give individuals the right to own and carry weapons, or does it restrict these rights only to members of the militia? Is this a protection of personal or collective rights? According to some "authorities," this amendment does not broadly grant citizens the right to keep and bear arms, but instead only allows arms to people who are to serve in a government-regulated militia. If all the amendment secured was the right to be a soldier in the military—a lonely, dangerous affair—could it really be considered one of the "great rights of mankind," worthy of constitutional protection? Once again, a brief look at the history of this amendment makes its meaning crystal clear.

Like many rights, the American right to have arms was inherited from England. In 1689, England adopted its Bill of Rights and endorsed the right of the people to bear arms, but that right was already centuries old. In the twelfth century, Henry II had ordered all freemen to have certain arms, and a century later, Henry III required all subjects aged fifteen to fifty to possess a weapon other than a knife. Crown officers would occasionally inspect subjects to ensure they were properly armed. The reason for this obligation was that England had no regular army or police force, so every man was charged with the duty of preserving the public peace by confronting and capturing suspicious persons and by suppressing riots. In the event of a crime, all men had to join in the "hue and cry"—calling forth assistance and joining in the pursuit of anyone who was resisting arrest or escaping from custody.

In 1671, Parliament infringed for the first time on the people's right to arms, passing a statute that deprived almost all Englishmen of it. Charles II further disarmed his Whig opposition, and in 1686, his successor, James II, enraged Protestants by banning their firearms but leaving Catholics armed. Such royal controls on weapons convinced Englishmen that they must be allowed to own firearms, and as a result, plans were set into motion to secure this right.

In the Glorious Revolution of 1689, James II was ousted and the usurper, William of Orange, promised to protect the Protestants' right to possess firearms. The final version of the law read, "That the Subjects which are Protestants may have Arms for their defence suitable to their Conditions, and as allowed by Law." England was about 98 percent Protestant at this time. This law prevented the king from ever disarming the population again because only Parliament could decide what is "allowed by law." The right to bear arms was resolutely established as one belonging to individuals.

Commonly cited by Americans, Blackstone stated in his *Commentaries* that the right "to have arms" was indispensable "to protect and maintain inviolate the three great and primary rights of personal security, personal liberty, and private property." James Burgh wrote at length about the right of the people to bear arms—more than one hundred pages, to be specific—praising the values of an armed population in preference to a standing army. "A militia-man," he wrote, "is a free citizen; a soldier, a slave for life." He argued that the ownership of firearms is what distinguished the free man from a slave, referring to arms as the "only true badges of liberty."

The Englishman's right to arms was cherished, and English settlers in America were guaranteed all rights of Englishmen. This included, of course, the laws of the English Bill of Rights, which protected the right of Protestants to have weapons for their own defense.

Americans came to loathe standing armies. Denouncements of George III were plentiful for using his military as a part of a plan to reduce the colonies to slavery. Jefferson vilified the king for using armed forces to carry out policies and attacked him in the Declaration of Independence for having kept "among us in time of peace, standing armies without the consent of our legislatures." Madison supported national control over state militias as an effective method of minimizing a standing army. George Mason and Jefferson agreed, arguing that well-prepared state militias under federal authority would keep the army small.

Thus, our first national constitution, the Articles of Confederation (1777), stated that each colony shall always keep up a well-regulated and disciplined militia, but it did not say anything specifically about the individual's right to be armed for his own defense or other purposes. Any such right would have to come from state law, and while several state constitutions stipulated militias, Pennsylvania's constitution of 1776 first used the phrase "the right to bear arms" despite the fact that it had no militia. Therefore, it had no military connotation or significance. A year later, Vermont used Pennsylvania's wording for its constitution. John Adams argued that the individual citizen had the right to arms for his defense, and this position was adopted by the Massachusetts constitution of 1780, which guaranteed the right of the people to simply "keep and bear arms" without limiting it to the militia. Virginia's Declaration of Rights of 1776 spoke only of having a well-regulated militia in place of a standing army, but it is worth considering that Virginians were to arm themselves and thus provide their own weapons when serving in the militia. North Carolina similarly defended the right to bear arms for the purpose of defending the state.

In 1792, Congress enacted the Uniform Militia Act, which called for militias to consist of "every free able-bodied male citizen of the respective states" aged eighteen to forty-five, and it stated that every militiaman should have his own weapons: "That every citizen so enrolled… shall…provide himself with a good musket or firelock, a sufficient bayonet, belt, two spare flints, and a knapsack, a pouch with a box therein to contain not less than twenty-four cartridges…each cartridge to contain a proper quantity of powder and ball."

Various amendments were proposed at the Pennsylvania ratifying convention that constituted a bill of rights, and one of the clauses addressed the issue of an individual's right to have arms: "That the people have a right to bear arms for the defense of themselves and their own State, or the United States, or for the purpose of killing game; and no law shall be passed for disarming the people or any of them, unless for crimes committed, or real danger of public injury from individuals." The provision then went on to reject standing armies and demand civil control over the military.

Luminaries in Massachusetts were of the same mind. Theodore Sedgwick declared that "a nation of freemen who know how to prize liberty and who have arms in their hands" could not be oppressed. Samuel Adams insisted that the Constitution should explicitly provide that it could never be interpreted to "prevent the people from keeping their own arms." Lexicographer Noah Webster agreed, stating that the federal government would be unable to enforce unreasonable laws because the "whole body of the people are armed." Zachariah Johnson informed the Virginia ratifying convention that the people's personal rights and freedoms were safe because they "are not to be disarmed of their weapons. They are left in full possession of them."

In 1789, James Madison proposed to the First Congress the amendments that would become the Bill of Rights. He included one that was based on his own state's constitution, and it read as follows: "The right of the people to keep and bear arms shall not be infringed; a well armed, and well regulated militia being the best security of a free country; but no person religiously scrupulous of being armed shall be compelled to render military service in person." Madison did not make the right of bearing arms conditional upon serving in the militia. In his personal letters, Madison referred to his amendments as "guards for private rights."

Similarly revealing is the fact that Madison originally proposed that the amendments be inserted directly into the Constitution at appropriate points. The clause guaranteeing the right to bear arms was to be placed directly after the guarantee of the writ of habeas corpus and the prohibition of bills of attainder, which granted personal liberties. As history would have it, Roger Sherman opposed the interlineations of the amendments because, he argued, it would give the mistaken impression that the Framers had signed a document that included clauses not of their creation. He and other House members felt the amendments should be lumped together at the end of the document: a proposition that won out, giving us the collective form we know today.

In the Virginia ratifying convention, Patrick Henry proclaimed that the people's only defense against an army controlled by Congress was the militia. "The great object," he roared, "is that every man be armed…. Every one who is able may have a gun." At this same ratifying convention, George Mason reminded those attending that the British had previously sought to disarm the colonials in an attempt to enslave them. "Who are the militia?" he asked. "They consist now of the whole people." Jefferson proposed that his state constitution should proclaim that "no freeman shall be debarred the use of arms."

Four states that recommended amendments to the Constitution urged one that guaranteed the right of individuals to have arms. New Hampshire was the first to propose such an amendment, and it said: "Congress shall never disarm any Citizen, unless such as are or have been in Actual Rebellion." New York proposed that the people "have a right to keep and bear arms" and that a well-regulated militia consisting of "the body of the people capable of bearing arms" is the "proper" defense of a free state. Rhode Island and North Carolina recommended similar amendments to the Constitution.

The right to bear arms can be regulated by public measures as to the kinds of weapons that are lawful and the circumstances under which weapons can be kept, but no law or rule can undermine the right itself. Militias were only possible because of armed populations that had the right to have arms. As we have now seen, the right does not depend on the existence of militias.

The rights granted by the Second Amendment have an illustrious history connected with the protection of freedom and opposition of tyranny and slavery. In today's society, the Second Amendment has proven invaluable to citizens for protecting themselves against criminals (disarming the people is a sure way to invigorate criminals, as they can get weapons regardless). Regarding its relation to opposition of the government, the Supreme Court said in 1951, in *Dennis vs. United States*, that Congress surely has the power to protect the government from armed rebellion, and that a right to revolution is without force where the government provides a system for peaceful, orderly change.

That notwithstanding, should Americans ever find themselves faced with an incurable government of totalitarian oppression, a government that has abandoned the very principles this nation was founded upon and that reconstituted a slavery like that of the past, then the people have the natural, inalienable right to change the government as they see fit, and the spirit of this amendment clearly applies.

Know Your Bill of Rights Essay

Give your understanding of the following statement:

"A well-regulated Militia, being necessary to the security of a free State…"

Know Your Bill of Rights

Essay

Why do you think the Framers felt a well-regulated militia is necessary to the security of a free state? Do you agree?

Know Your Bill of Rights Essay

What type of attacks or dangers would a well-regulated militia protect against?

Know Your Bill of Rights Essay

Give your understanding of the following statement:

"...the right of the people to keep and bear Arms, shall not be infringed."

Know Your Bill of Rights

Essay

Give three specific examples of freedoms or rights this clause gives you and others.

Know Your Bill of Rights

Essay

Give three specific examples of restrictions this clause puts on the government.

Know Your Bill of Rights Essay

Give three specific examples of ways the government could violate this clause.

Know Your Bill of Rights

Essay

Why do you think this clause is important? Do you agree with this clause? If not, explain.

THE THIRD AMENDMENT KEY WORDS DRILL

Purpose of this drill:

The purpose of this drill is to ensure you understand the basic words you will be coming across while studying the Third Amendment of the Bill of Rights.

How this drill is done:

This drill is done with another person. Both people are to read the drill's questions and answers before starting the drill.

The person asking the questions is the "coach," and the person answering is the "student." The coach asks the student the question, and the student answers it. The answer does not have to be word-for-word; just the concept must be correct.

If the student gets a question incorrect, the coach shows him or her the answer. The coach then has the student explain the answer in his or her own words. Once the student has it in his or her own words, the coach re-asks the question. The coach then continues with the next question. Once they've gone through all the questions, they start again from the beginning.

How to pass this drill:

The student is done with the drill when he or she can answer all the questions correctly, from the first to the last, without missing any.

The point of this drill is not for you to just memorize the answers to the questions, it is to help you actually understand the information.

Note:

Words often have several meanings. The definitions used in this drill only give the meaning that the word has as it is used in this workbook. To get the full understanding of each word, look at its other definitions in a dictionary.

QUESTIONS:

1. **What does *quarter* mean?**

    To provide a place to live in for some period of time.

    Example sentence: They quartered the student for three months.

2. **What is *consent*?**

    Acceptance of or agreement to something proposed or desired by another.

3. **What does *nor* mean?**

    And not.

    Example sentence: Nobody shall enter nor shall they take pictures.

4. **What is a *manner*?**

    The way in which something is done or happens.

5. **What does *prescribe* mean?**

    To say with authority that a course of action should be taken; to lay down a rule.

END OF DRILL

★ ★ ★

The Bill of Rights
The Third Amendment

No Soldier shall, in time of peace be quartered in any house, without the consent of the Owner, nor in time of war, but in a manner to be prescribed by law.

Know Your Bill of Rights Essay

Give your understanding of the following statement:

"No Soldier shall, in time of peace be quartered in any house, without the consent of the Owner…"

Know Your Bill of Rights Essay

Give your understanding of the following statement:

"…nor in time of war, but in a manner to be prescribed by law."

Know Your Bill of Rights

Essay

Why do you think this clause is important in today's society? Do you agree with this clause? If not, explain.

The Fourth Amendment Key Words Drill

Purpose of this drill:

The purpose of this drill is to ensure you understand the basic words you will be coming across while studying the Fourth Amendment of the Bill of Rights.

How this drill is done:

This drill is done with another person. Both people are to read the drill's questions and answers before starting the drill.

The person asking the questions is the "coach," and the person answering is the "student." The coach asks the student the question, and the student answers it. The answer does not have to be word-for-word; just the concept must be correct.

If the student gets a question incorrect, the coach shows him or her the answer. The coach then has the student explain the answer in his or her own words. Once the student has it in his or her own words, the coach re-asks the question. The coach then continues with the next question. Once they've gone through all the questions, they start again from the beginning.

How to pass this drill:

The student is done with the drill when he or she can answer all the questions correctly, from the first to the last, without missing any.

The point of this drill is not for you to just memorize the answers to the questions, it is to help you actually understand the information.

Note:

Words often have several meanings. The definitions used in this drill only give the meaning that the word has as it is used in this workbook. To get the full understanding of each word, look at its other definitions in a dictionary.

QUESTIONS:

1. **What does *secure* mean?**

    Free from or not exposed to danger, risk, harm or loss; safe.

2. **What are *papers*?**

    A document or documents showing somebody's identity or legal status.

3. **What is a *person*?**

    The body of a living human being, sometimes including the clothes being worn.

4. **What are *effects*?**

    Somebody's personal possessions or the things that somebody is carrying on him or her.

5. **What is *common sense*?**

    Good judgment based on a simple understanding of the facts, not on special knowledge or training.

6. **What does *unreasonable* mean?**

    Exceeding what is acceptable and in agreement with common sense; claiming or insisting on more than is appropriate.

7. **What is *seizure*?**

    The act of taking something by force or the legal taking of something that belongs to somebody else.

8. **What does *violate* mean?**

    To break or ignore a law, agreement, etc.

9. **What is an *oath*?**

    A formal and legally binding promise of the truth of one's words or that one will do as one says, usually calling upon God as a witness.

END OF DRILL

★ ★ ★

The Bill of Rights
The Fourth Amendment

The right of the people to be secure in their persons, houses, papers, and effects, against unreasonable searches and seizures, shall not be violated, and no Warrants shall issue, but upon probable cause, supported by Oath or affirmation, and particularly describing the place to be searched, and the persons or things to be seized.

★ ★ ★

The Story Behind The Fourth Amendment

"Where an excess of power prevails, property of no sort is duly respected. No man is safe in his opinions, his person, his faculties, or his possessions."

– *James Madison*

The right for citizens to be secure against unreasonable searches and seizures was almost nonexistent before the American Revolution. British policies granted no privacy of households and places of business, especially when royal revenues were involved. "No taxation without representation" was a slogan of the mid-1700s that summarized a primary grievance of the colonists and one of the major causes of the Revolution. British enforcements of tax policies by general searches also deeply embittered Americans, giving rise to concerns that later found expression in the Fourth Amendment.

This Amendment, however, was a constitutional embodiment and expansion of an earlier combination of the Magna Carta with the belief that "a man's house is his castle"—a maxim that dates back at least to the early sixteenth century—that was repeated so often that it became a cliché. Ironically, the Magna Carta was a feudal document that protected the barons and never was meant as a constitution for everyone. Regardless, its first link to the privacy of one's own home goes back to 1589 when Robert Beale, the clerk of the Privy Council, cited Chapter 39 of the Magna Carta as a basis for objecting to agents of the prerogative court entering into subjects' houses, invading and damaging their belongings, and taking whatever they considered evidence.

Despite the fact that Beale's argument was historically unsound, what the Magna Carta actually said was not as important what people thought it said or, rather, what it had come to mean. What also mattered was the inspiring message of freedom for the common subjects. In a heartfelt speech to Parliament in 1763, William Pitt declared: "The poorest man may, in his cottage, bid defiance to all the forces of the Crown. It may be frail; its roof may shake; the wind may blow through it; the storm may enter; the rain may enter; but the King of England may not enter; all his force dares not cross the threshold of the ruined tenement."

Sir Edmund Coke's *Institutes of the Lawes of England* was one of the most influential writings on the belief that a legitimate search can only be authorized by a legal writ that specifies the persons and places to be searched. Americans regarded Coke as the foremost authority on English law, and his influence further validated the belief that the Magna Carta outlawed general warrants based on mere suspicion.

In his book *The History of the Pleas of the Crown*, Sir Matthew Hale denounced warrants that did not name the persons wanted for crime or the places to be searched for evidence of theft. He even spoke of what would later be known as probable cause, arguing that the person seeking a warrant should be examined under oath by a judge to verify the suspicions had reasonable grounds.

Beale, Coke, and Hale started a rhetorical tradition against general warrants and searches, one joined by other luminaries such as Serjeant-at-Law William Hawkins and Sir William Blackstone, but the dissemination of such ideas had little practical effect.

English law was full of enactments that used general searches and warrants for enforcement, including those used to collect many different taxes; measures punishing theft; measures preventing illegal imports, counterfeiting, and unlicensed manufacturing; and many others. Warrants were nearly unlimited in scope and granted few exceptions, allowing officers to search wherever and seize whatever they pleased.

Colonial search and seizure practices mirrored Britain's: until 1750, only general warrants were issued. American colonists were granted even less privacy than Britons because, while adapting English models, the Americans ignored exceptions granted in England. Thus, American officers executing searches and seizures could exercise their powers without any restraints. The Fourth Amendment did not have colonial precedents; it rejected them.

If an officer or informant merely reported a violation of the law or that he suspected such, not that a particular person had committed a crime or a place had evidence of it, a magistrate issued a warrant. No law obligated the magistrate to interrogate the seeker of the warrant to determine the validity of the claims. To the contrary, the magistrate had an obligation to give the warrant rather than deny the request because of lack of specificity as to persons or places.

American colonials had to wait until 1756 for the first legislative breakthrough on this subject. Delivered by the province of Massachusetts, legislation was passed that abandoned general warrants in favor of warrants based on some level of specificity, a move that William Cuddihy referred to as the "statutory prototypes of the Fourth Amendment."

This legislation came in the midst of considerable public outcry against the excise act of 1754, which authorized tax collectors to grill any subject, under oath, on the types and amounts of alcohol consumed in his home in the past year and then to tax it by the gallon. Provincial impost laws relied on general searches and warrants for enforcement, and these were so unpopular that mobs threatened impost officers who tried to collect taxes on imports for which duties had not yet been paid. Writs of assistance were another type of controversial general warrant that allowed a crown official to order the assistance of a peace officer and, if necessary, all nearby subjects, to help execute a writ, such as the search for and seizure of uncustomed goods. Equally disagreeable were general warrants that authorized impressment gangs to kidnap able-bodied men and enlist them in the Royal Navy.

These practices generated much animosity, and statutes enacted in 1756 sought to quiet it. The enactments required informants to swear under oath that they knew a crime had occurred in the place stated. However, magistrates made no judgment as to whether there were reasonable grounds for a warrant—the law simply required the informant to swear he had "just cause" for his sworn statement. The new measures also required officers to conduct searches in the daytime, restricted the searches to only the locations specified, and limited seizures to objects monitored by the statute being enforced by the warrant.

When King George II died in 1760, all writs of assistance were set to expire six months after his death, at which time new writs would have to be obtained from the new sovereign. Within weeks of the king's death, the writs were challenged by a group of sixty-three Boston merchants, represented by the fiery attorney James Otis, Jr. Otis famously argued against the writs of assistance twice in 1761. Otis called the writ of assistance an instrument of "slavery," "villainy," and "arbitrary power, the most destructive of English liberty and [of] the fundamental principles of the constitution." He claimed that such writs were a violation of natural rights and thus were void along with any authorizations of the writs by Parliament, and despite the fact that his arguments were historically flawed, he was making history. His impassioned rhetoric made a lasting impression on a young John Adams, who was present in the courtroom. Fifty-six years later, Adams wrote, "Otis was a flame of Fire!...Then and there was the first scene of the first Act of Opposition to the arbitrary Claims of Great Britain. Then and there the child of Independance [sic] was born." Otis's speech in 1761 directly influenced Adams's framing of Article XIV of the Massachusetts Declaration of Rights of 1780, which directly influenced Madison's later proposition that became the Fourth Amendment.

Otis lost his case and writs were issued, but he had ignited a cause for Americans and stirred controversy. In 1763, John Wilkes delivered a scathing criticism of George III in the forty-fifth edition of his weekly publication, *The North Briton*. The English government retaliated in a draconian fashion, issuing general search warrants for the arrest of everyone connected with the tract. Crown officers scoured printer's shops and houses and arrested forty-nine people, including Wilkes, his printer and publisher, a member of Parliament, and booksellers. The House of Commons voted that Wilkes's *The North Briton No. 45* was seditious libel and exiled him.

The government soon learned, however, that Wilkes was a capable, persistent adversary. He quickly filed suits for trespass against everyone connected with the warrant that led to his capture, and other victims followed with suits of their own for trespass and false imprisonment. The Wilkes case was a sensational controversy and transformed Wilkes into a popular idol, an embodiment of liberty to Englishmen at home and in the New World.

"Wilkes and Liberty" became a motto patriots of American causes used, and the Fourth Amendment, as well as the First and Fifth, owe something to the Wilkes cases. In one case, the government appealed to the highest criminal court in England, the King's Bench, and its chief justice, Lord Mansfield, upheld the ruling that the Wilkes warrants were unjustified and illegal. Mansfield felt that the "magistrate ought to judge; and should give certain directions to the officer"—a base for what later became probable cause. In the end, the Wilkes fiasco cost the government nearly one hundred thousand pounds in costs and judgments—the equivalent of about twenty-five million in today's dollars.

In 1766, after landmark judicial decisions and much debate on the legality of general search warrants, the House of Commons passed three resolutions, not laws, that repudiated general warrants in all cases involving arrests but condemned searches for illegal writings only when in connections of crimes of seditious libel. Though it was progress, the reforms from 1763 to 1766 still conformed to the English common-law understanding of search and seizure: general searches did not violate a subject's liberties so long as they were executed in accordance with laws laid down by Parliament.

About twenty years later, Madison, speaking in the First Congress to recommend amendments that would become the Bill of Rights, knew that such unlimited legislative power was a great danger to the people's liberties. In Britain, he said, "they have gone no farther than to raise a barrier against the power of the Crown; the power of the Legislature is left altogether infinite."

The Townshend Acts that were passed in 1767 further stoked the fires of controversy over writs of assistance in the colonies, turning what was a localized uproar mainly in Boston into a continent-wide dispute. Parliament was ordering colonial courts to issue writs of assistance, and only two of the colonies that had previously experienced the writs would continue issuing them.

Chief Justice Jonathan Trumbull of Connecticut and Judge Roger Sherman of Connecticut would not allow themselves to be rushed into complying with Parliament's demands. Chief Justice William Allen of Pennsylvania outright declared that he had no legal authority to issue the writs as is, and even after the urging of Attorney General William de Grey of England, refused to grant general writs and would only issue "particular writs whenever they are applied for on oath." A South Carolina judge refused to issue the writ, stating it violated safeties granted to subjects by the Magna Carta. Virginia issued writs of assistance in 1769, but the process was hamstrung by the court's requirement that the agent swear on oath in favor of his suspicion and by the granting of the writs only on special occasion and for a limited time.

From 1761 to 1776, the tide of legal opinion on general searches and seizures in the colonies was drifting away from the common-law precedent inherited from England, with recommendations of the use of specific warrants in certain cases finding their way into law books and manuals. Nevertheless, during this time, American judges continued to rely on general warrants in actual practice. Despite appeals to the Magna Carta as grounds for rejecting British orders of general searches, colonial legislatures and judicatures used general search warrants that read just like writs of assistance to enforce their own laws.

This hypocrisy would change, however. While embroiled in the Revolution, Americans created some of the most important and radical constitutional achievements in history. One was the new benchmarks that emerged on the subject of searches and seizures, providing the models for the Fourth Amendment.

Virginia, for instance, included the following in its Declaration of Rights, adopted on June 12, 1776: "That general warrants, whereby any officer or messenger may be commanded to search suspected places without evidence of a fact committed, or to seize any person or persons not named, or whose offence is not particularly described and supported by evidence, are grievous and oppressive, and ought not to be granted." This article was a pioneering step in the direction of specific warrants, despite its obvious shortcomings, such as its irresolute "ought not," its condemnation of general warrants as "grievous" but not illegal, its failure to require specificity as to things to be seized, and the lack of prohibition of the use of general warrants.

In August 1776, Pennsylvania adopted its Declaration of Rights, which was influenced by Virginia's but still original in many ways, pushing the frontier of specific warrants further. Its tenth article read: "That the people have a right to hold themselves, their houses, papers, and possessions free from search and seizure, and therefore warrants without oaths or affirmations first made, affording a sufficient foundation for them, and whereby any officer or messenger may be commanded or required to search suspected places, or to seize any person or persons, his or their property, not particularly described, are contrary to that right, and ought not to be granted." This provision was memorable in that it asserted a right of the people instead of merely renouncing general searches, required specificity as to things seized, and was the first to require a warrant to be issued to an informant to swear or affirm that he had "sufficient foundation" for his information being given. An obvious drawback was, again, the usage of the weak "ought not to be granted" wording and the lack of prohibition of the denounced violations.

Delaware's Declaration of Rights of 1776 copied Maryland and Pennsylvania's clause on search and seizure. It was stunted in its own ways, omitting the assertion of a right of the people and the requirement for specificity regarding things to be seized, but its major contribution was the first pronouncement of warrants not meeting the constitutional criteria as illegal.

New Hampshire's Declaration of Rights of 1784 copied Massachusetts's, which provided the most important statement of the right, as it is the one the Fourth Amendment most resembles. Massachusetts's search and seizure provision was the work of John Adams, who had been so strongly moved by Otis's monumental speech nearly twenty years earlier. Through Adams, Article XIV of the Massachusetts Declaration of Rights declared:

"Every subject has a right to be secure from all unreasonable searches, and seizures of his person, his houses, his papers, and all his possessions. All warrants, therefore, are contrary to this right, if the cause or foundation of them be not previously supported by oath or affirmation; and if the order in the warrant to the civil officer, to make search in suspected places, to arrest one or more suspected persons, or to seize their property, be not accompanied with a special designation of the person or objects of search, arrest, or seizure: and no warrant ought to be issued but in cases and with the formalities, prescribed by the laws."

Adams's draft was striking. It declared a constitutional right of the people, was the first to use the phrase "unreasonable searches and seizures," and required a sworn statement of cause or foundation for the warrant. The only obvious fault is that it oddly omitted a requirement that the search, arrest, or seizure be limited to a specific location.

When Madison began his fight in the House for amendments protecting personal liberties, he was without a single supporter. He intended to convince the great body of Americans who withheld their approval of the Constitution because they felt it should secure them against governmental abuse.

When he proposed an amendment on searches and seizures, he opted for granting the maximum protection possible at the time: "The rights of the people to be secured in their persons, their houses, and their other property, from all unreasonable searches and seizures, shall not be violated by warrants issued without probable cause, supported by oath or affirmation, or not particularly describing the places to be searched, or the persons or things to be seized."

He dropped the questionable "ought not" for the assertive "shall not," he contributed the significant phrase "probable cause," and above all, he granted rights to the people, not just restrictions on the government.

After deliberations, the House adopted Madison's wording with only two minor changes: "rights" became "right," and "secured" became "secure." The final wording was as follows: "The right of the people to be secure in their persons, houses, papers, and effects, against unreasonable searches and seizures, shall not be violated, and no Warrants shall issue, but upon probable cause, supported by Oath or affirmation, and particularly describing the place to be searched, and the persons or things to be seized."

The Fourth Amendment was an unprecedented liberalization of search and seizure law, using the broadest language ever known at the time. It was a bold milestone in the advancement of the common people from slaves of the crown to sovereign individuals who were not subject to the oppressive whims of ill-intentioned "authorities." While it failed to stipulate a penalty for an illegal search or seizure or the presentation of illegally seized goods as evidence, while the words "probable" and "unreasonable" can have subjective meanings attached, and while it does not specify the liabilities of those officers who might violate it, its spirit is clear when viewed in the right historical context, and we count on our judicial and legislative officials to keep its application true to the original intent.

Know Your Bill of Rights Essay

Give your understanding of the following statement:

"The right of the people to be secure in their persons, houses, papers, and effects, against unreasonable searches and seizures, shall not be violated…"

Know Your Bill of Rights

Essay

Give three specific examples of freedoms or rights this clause gives you and others.

Know Your Bill of Rights Essay

Give three specific examples of restrictions this clause puts on the government.

Know Your Bill of Rights

Essay

Give three specific examples of ways the government could violate this clause.

Know Your Bill of Rights

Essay

Why do you think this clause is important in today's society? Do you agree with this clause? If not, explain.

Know Your Bill of Rights

Essay

Give your understanding of the following statement:

"…and no Warrants shall issue, but upon probable cause, supported by Oath or affirmation, and particularly describing the place to be searched, and the persons or things to be seized."

Know Your Bill of Rights

Essay

Give three specific examples of freedoms or rights this clause gives you and others.

Know Your Bill of Rights

Essay

Give three specific examples of restrictions this clause puts on the government or the people.

Know Your Bill of Rights

Essay

Give three specific examples of ways the government or the people could violate this clause.

Know Your Bill of Rights

Essay

Why do you think this clause is important in today's society? Do you agree with this clause? If not, explain.

The Fifth Amendment Key Words Drill

Purpose of this drill:

The purpose of this drill is to ensure you understand the basic words you will be coming across while studying the Fifth Amendment of the Bill of Rights.

How this drill is done:

This drill is done with another person. Both people are to read the drill's questions and answers before starting the drill.

The person asking the questions is the "coach," and the person answering is the "student." The coach asks the student the question, and the student answers it. The answer does not have to be word-for-word; just the concept must be correct.

If the student gets a question incorrect, the coach shows him or her the answer. The coach then has the student explain the answer in his or her own words. Once the student has it in his or her own words, the coach re-asks the question. The coach then continues with the next question. Once they've gone through all the questions, they start again from the beginning.

How to pass this drill:

The student is done with the drill when he or she can answer all the questions correctly, from the first to the last, without missing any.

The point of this drill is not for you to just memorize the answers to the questions, it is to help you actually understand the information.

Note:

Words often have several meanings. The definitions used in this drill only give the meaning that the word has as it is used in this workbook. To get the full understanding of each word, look at its other definitions in a dictionary.

QUESTIONS:

1. **What does *capital* mean?**

    Involving or bringing about punishment by death.

2. **What does *infamous* mean?**

    Punishable by severe measures, such as death, long imprisonment or loss of rights.

3. **What does *subject (to)* mean?**

    To cause to undergo the action of something specified.

4. **What does *compel* mean?**

    To drive, urge or force by physical, legal, social or moral means.

5. **What is *liberty*?**

    Freedom from restraint or control regarding one's body, actions or mind.

6. **What does *deprive* mean?**

    To take something away from somebody.

7. **What does *due* mean?**

    Meeting all the necessary requirements and thus proper and appropriate to the situation.

8. **What does *public* mean?**

    Having to do with a nation, state or community; extending to a whole people, as opposed to private, which indicates what belongs to an individual, group or company.

9. **What does *just* mean?**

    Right or fair.

10. **What is *compensation*?**

    An amount of money or something else given to pay for loss, damage or work done.

END OF DRILL

★ ★ ★

THE BILL OF RIGHTS
THE FIFTH AMENDMENT

No person shall be held to answer for a capital, or otherwise infamous crime, unless on a presentment or indictment of a Grand Jury, except in cases arising in the land or naval forces, or in the Militia, when in actual service in time of War or public danger; nor shall any person be subject for the same offence to be twice put in jeopardy of life or limb; nor shall be compelled in any criminal case to be a witness against himself, nor be deprived of life, liberty, or property, without due process of law; nor shall private property be taken for public use, without just compensation.

★ ★ ★

THE STORY BEHIND THE FIFTH AMENDMENT

"The 5th Amendment is an old friend and a good friend. It is one of the great landmarks in men's struggle to be free of tyranny, to be decent and civilized."

– William O. Douglas

The Bill of Rights indicated a preoccupation with the subject of criminal justice—with good reason. The Framers had in mind much history that has been largely forgotten today: without fair and standardized protections for those accused of crimes, individual liberty was impossible. Since the beginning of history, tyrants have used criminal law to crush opposition, nonconformists, and undesirable minorities. Indeed, one's home could not be his castle, his property be his own, or his rights to expression and conscience be intact if he could be searched, arrested, judged, or imprisoned in inconsistent or unjust ways.

THE RIGHT AGAINST SELF-INCRIMINATION

As Justice Felix Frankfurter said, "The privilege against self-incrimination is a specific provision of which it is peculiarly true that 'a page of history is worth a volume of logic.'" This history of the right against self-incrimination, however, is complex and multifaceted. The American versions of the right derive mainly from the common-law system of justice inherited from England. The English origins, however, extend beyond the boundaries of law and wind a path through the religious, political, and constitutional issues England was facing during the sixteenth and seventeenth centuries: the clashes between Parliament and king, between the crown and pope, between Anglicanism and Puritanism, between arbitrary rule and limited government, and between freedom of conscience and punishment of heresy and sedition.

Even when restricting our view to the realm of law alone, the history of the right also draws from the similarly broad issues of the battle for supremacy between the adversarial and inquisitorial systems of justice, between the royal prerogative and common law, and between the common law and its ecclesiastical and civil law opponents.

This right's origin can be traced back to the use of the common law's accusatory system and of rival systems that followed inquisitorial procedures. Toward the end of the sixteenth century, all criminal courts in England regularly sought to compel self-incriminatory disclosures from those suspected of or charged with the commission of a crime. Despite this and other harsh procedures, the accusatory system was fairer than the inquisitional system, which was a hopeless travesty of justice that commonly meant a trial based on mere rumor or suspicion, the oath ex officio, secrecy, lack of confrontation with accusers, confessions coerced by torture, and magistrates that paradoxically were to accuse and prosecute while acting as the "judge." "Abandon all hope, ye who enter here" summed up the chances of a person accused under inquisitorial procedures.

These draconian judicial methods were introduced by English ecclesiastical courts as an "efficient" way to deal with heresy. Persons were merely suspected of "heretical opinions," "seditious books," or "conspiracies," and summoned before the Court of High Commission without any knowledge of the accusation against them or who their accusers were. They were then denied due process of law as dictated by common law and required to take an oath to truthfully answer all questions that would seek to prove guilt for crimes still uncharged and undisclosed. A refusal to take the oath or to answer inquiries meant a sentence for contempt and an invitation for Star Chamber proceedings, while truthful responses to questions often meant conviction of religious or political crimes and coercion to supply evidence against accomplices. To take the oath and lie was to sin against the Scriptures and to open one to conviction for perjury.

Puritan common lawyers developed a courageous argument against such gross violations of due process, and it was that such an oath, although approved by the sovereign, was unconstitutional because it violated the Magna Carta, which limited even the royal prerogative. This argument was one of the first to hold up the Magna Carta as the icon and source of English constitutional freedom.

A later generation carried this torch and claimed "that by the Statutes of the Magna Carta… for a man to accuse himself was and is utterly inhibited" in support of the belief that one is not obligated to answer all questions even after being accused of a crime.

A deep hostility was growing between the systems of common law and canon law, and in the 1630s, the High Commission and the Star Chamber, which used similarly inquisitorial procedures, had reached the height of their powers. But in 1637, Puritan dissident John Lilburne refused the oath. His opposition to self-incrimination was widely publicized and turned England's attention to the unfairness and illegality of such measures. In 1641, the Long Parliament, full of common lawyers and Puritans, denounced the sentences handed down to Lilburne and others, dissolved the Star Chamber and the High Commission, and prohibited the use of any oath requiring one "to confess or to accuse himself or herself of any crime."

Common-law courts, however, continued to bully witnesses into answering incriminating questions. Nevertheless, the concept of right against self-incrimination was securely installed in the writings of Coke, tirelessly popularized by Lilburne and the Levellers, and permanently connected with the Magna Carta. By the early eighteenth century, the criminally accused were treated fairer than ever before in England. Coercing prisoners for answers had died out; they were no longer put on the stand to face interrogation, and they had no obligation to answer incriminating questions. In his *Law of Evidence* (1756), Lord Chief Baron Geoffrey Gilbert wrote that while a confession is the best evidence of guilt, "this Confession must be voluntary and without compulsion; for our Law… will not force any Man to accuse himself; and in this we do certainly follow that Law of Nature," which commands self-preservation.

With the development of this right came other procedures that installed fairness for the criminally accused, such as the principle of innocence until proven guilty and that the burden of proof should rest on the prosecution, and the ideas that a man's home should not be broken into and ransacked for evidence, that torture or cruelty used to compel confession is unjust and illegal, and that one has a right to counsel and to have witnesses testify on his behalf.

Above all, the right against self-incrimination was intimately associated with freedom of speech and religion, as it was originated by those who were convicted of religious crimes such as heresy, schism, and nonconformity and later, of political crimes such as treason, seditious libel, and violation of parliamentary privilege. It was less a protection of the guilty or innocent than a protector of political and religious freedom, and it was an established tradition by the eighteenth century.

Despite the colonies' inheritance of all just mentioned, the right had to be re-won in every colony under circumstances similar to those that were its catalyst in England. In the middle of the seventeenth century, many citizens of the colonies, faced with inquisitorial tactics of the prerogative court of the governor and council, refused to answer incriminatory inquiries in cases dealing with political affairs.

But as American law incorporated more English common law and the American legal profession grew in size, competence, and importance, Americans came to recognize the right.

When James Madison proposed his amendments that became the Bill of Rights, no other state had a self-incrimination clause worded as generously as his: "No person shall be subject, except in cases of impeachment, to more than one punishment or trial for the same offense; nor shall be compelled to be a witness against himself; nor be deprived of life, liberty, or property, where it may be necessary for public use, without a just compensation."

Madison's proposal applied to civil and criminal proceedings and in theory to any stage of a legal investigation, whether an initial examination in a criminal case or the giving of a deposition in a civil one. It applied to any governmental inquiry, not just judicial proceedings. The statement that nobody shall be compelled to be a witness against himself also protected one from being forced to give any testimony that would expose one to public humiliation or censure or other harm to name or reputation. Madison's proposal also protected witnesses who were called to give testimony for either party in that they could not be compelled to give testimony that might open them to criminal prosecution or civil penalties. In drafting this amendment, Madison went beyond the recommendations of the states to provide very broad application.

George Mason, however, deserves credit for constitutionalizing the old English rule that a person "cannot be compelled to give evidence against himself." Virginia adopted that phrasing as section 8 of its Declaration of Rights of 1776, but its protection was technically granted only to the criminally accused. In actual practice, however, Virginia's courts extended the right against self-incrimination to embrace all stages of equity and common-law proceedings and also allowed witnesses and defendants to invoke the right. If one's disclosures in any stage of any legal proceeding could make him liable to legal penalty, he could call on this right to silence. He could also invoke the right if his disclosures could not lead to prosecution but to infamy and disgrace, shielding him from public defamation.

Other states modeled their own declarations of rights after Virginia's, and it served as a foundation of the Bill of Rights itself, making it one of America's most influential constitutional documents. The eight states that added separate bills of rights to their constitutions upheld the right against self-incrimination, and every one used language almost identical to Virginia's section 8, stating that nobody can be "compelled to give evidence against himself."

In opposition to a provision of the Judiciary Act of 1789, Senator William Maclay of Pennsylvania asserted that "extorting evidence from any person was a species of torture.... [H]ere was an attempt to exercise a tyranny of the same kind over the mind. The conscience was to be put on the rack; that forcing oaths or evidence from men, I consider equally tyrannical as extorting evidence by torture."

The earliest state and federal cases after the adoption of the Fifth Amendment also showed that the right to not be a witness against oneself embraced, not restricted, the common law precedent that, at least in criminal cases, one was protected against being compelled to produce any injurious evidence, including that which would bring infamy. State courts of the time supported the extension of the right to protect against self-infamy as well as self-incrimination, but the self-infamy rule fell into obscurity.

Justice Abe Fortas communicated the spirit of the amendment succinctly when he said the following: "The principle that a man is not obligated to furnish the state with ammunition to use against him is basic to this conception." The state must defend itself, he acknowledged, and punish lawbreakers within the limits of accepted procedure. "But it has no right to compel the sovereign individual to surrender or impair his right of self-defense." The underlying principle of the Fifth Amendment "is intangible, it is true; but so is liberty, and so is man's immortal soul. A man may be punished, even put to death, by the state; but...he should not be made to prostrate himself before its majesty. Mea culpa belongs to a man and his God. It is a plea that cannot be exacted from free men by human authority. To require it is to insist that the state is the superior of the individuals who compose it, instead of their instrument."

The Fifth Amendment is a crucial element of the procedures that ensure the survival of our most treasured rights. The Framers believed deeply in a system of criminal justice that not only took significant precautions to avoid convicting the innocent but that also showed compassion and concern for the criminal offender.

The Fifth Amendment reflects the principle that, in a free society that respects the individual, the application of just procedures to determine guilt or innocence, in which the accused is to make no unwilling contributions, is more important than exacting punishment on the guilty.

THE DOUBLE JEOPARDY CLAUSE

The legal principle that a person should not be tried more than once for the same offense can be found in early legal systems, including Roman, Talmudic, and canon law. In his *Digest*, the Emperor Justinian commanded government not to allow "the same person to be again accused of crime of which he had been acquitted." The King James Version of the Bible stated that "affliction shall not rise up a second time."

Since the time of Coke, the idea of double jeopardy in England had been primarily connected with criminal cases, and it allowed a defendant to plead that because he had been tried previously for the same offense, he was immune from further prosecution for it. Regardless of whether he was previously acquitted or convicted, it was illegal to try him again for the same crime. In a case of 1696, the King's Bench—England's highest criminal court—affirmed the right when it acquitted defendants charged with larceny because they had been acquitted of earlier charges of breaking and entering for the same crime. Though they faced different charges than before, the court's ruling said the defendants could not be indicted for larceny or on any charge "for the same fact" or deed.

Sir William Blackstone in his *Commentaries* summarized the matter when he asserted that the plea of previous acquittal was "grounded on this universal maxim of the common law of England, that no man is to be brought into jeopardy of his life, more than once, for the same offence." In Coke and Blackstone, the right against double jeopardy applied only to felony cases, but a maxim became popular that interpreted the right much more broadly: "It is a rule of law that a man shall not be twice vexed for one and the same cause."

In the American colonies, the protection against double jeopardy was widely accepted and not restricted to jeopardy of life or only to felony cases. The Massachusetts Body of Liberties of 1641 generously declared, "No man shall be twice sentenced by civil justice for one and the same crime, offense, or trespass." But when Massachusetts codified its laws in 1648, it limited the right against double jeopardy to criminal cases by stipulating that all actions in "criminal causes" shall be recorded and "not afterwards brought again to the vexation of any man." This phrasing was the model for similar declarations in other colonies.

Declarations that all free people possessed the rights of Englishmen living in England, of course granting protection against double jeopardy, were common among the colonies. New Hampshire, however, was the first state to provide in its constitution of 1784 protection against double jeopardy by forbidding a second trial for anyone previously found not guilty of a particular offense. In 1788, Pennsylvania's high court stated that "no man shall be twice put in jeopardy for the same offense."

When James Madison introduced his amendments that became the Bill of Rights to the First Congress, he proposed: "No person shall be subject, except in case of impeachment, to more than one trial or one punishment for the same offence...." Considering the fact that only two states had recommended such protection, Madison's proposal shows how responsibly he approached the task of framing the amendments, going far beyond what was necessary to merely quell Anti-Federalist agitations.

The House adopted Madison's proposal, but the Senate deleted the last half of it, replacing it with "be twice put in jeopardy of life and limb in any public prosecution." After a joint conference committee's review, the closing words of "in any public prosecution" were struck.

There is no record of the debate, so we cannot be sure whether the clause was to follow the established understanding of double jeopardy despite the use of "life and limb," which would seem to restrict it only to felony cases. It is fair to assume, however, that "limb" was not used literally, unless the Framers contemplated the possibility that punishment might one day involve tearing criminals apart, a sure violation of the Eighth Amendment.

The Fifth Amendment is, unfortunately, unclear as to exact meaning and scope, but the history of the right does lend insight into the spirit in which it was proposed.

Know Your Bill of Rights

Essay

Give your understanding of the following statement:

"No person shall be held to answer for a capital, or otherwise infamous crime, unless on a presentment or indictment of a Grand Jury…"

Know Your Bill of Rights

Essay

Give three specific examples of freedoms or rights this clause gives you and others.

Know Your Bill of Rights Essay

Give three specific examples of restrictions this clause puts on the government.

Know Your Bill of Rights

Essay

Give three specific examples of ways the government could violate this clause.

Know Your Bill of Rights

Essay

Why do you think this clause is important in today's society? Do you agree with this clause? If not, explain.

Know Your Bill of Rights

Essay

Give your understanding of the following statement:

"…except in cases arising in the land or naval forces, or in the Militia, when in actual service in time of War or public danger…"

Know Your Bill of Rights Essay

Give your understanding of the following statement:

"...nor shall any person be subject for the same offence to be twice put in jeopardy of life or limb..."

Know Your Bill of Rights

Essay

Why do you think this clause is important in today's society? Do you agree with this clause? If not, explain.

Know Your Bill of Rights Essay

Give your understanding of the following statement:

"…nor shall be compelled in any criminal case to be a witness against himself…"

Know Your Bill of Rights

Essay

Give three specific examples of freedoms or rights this clause gives you and others.

Know Your Bill of Rights

Essay

Give three specific examples of restrictions this clause puts on the government.

Know Your Bill of Rights

Essay

Give three specific examples of ways the government could violate this clause.

Know Your Bill of Rights

Essay

Why do you think this clause is important in today's society? Do you agree with this clause? If not, explain.

Know Your Bill of Rights Essay

Give your understanding of the following statement:

"**…nor be deprived of life, liberty, or property, without due process of law…**"

Know Your Bill of Rights Essay

Give three specific examples of freedoms or rights this clause gives you and others.

Know Your Bill of Rights Essay

Give three specific examples of restrictions this clause puts on the government.

Know Your Bill of Rights Essay

Give three specific examples of ways the government could violate this clause.

Know Your Bill of Rights

Essay

Why do you think this clause is important in today's society? Do you agree with this clause? If not, explain.

Know Your Bill of Rights Essay

Give your understanding of the following statement:

"…nor shall private property be taken for public use, without just compensation."

Know Your Bill of Rights

Essay

Give three specific examples of freedoms or rights this clause gives you and others.

Know Your Bill of Rights Essay

Give three specific examples of restrictions this clause puts on the government.

Know Your Bill of Rights

Essay

Give three specific examples of ways the government could violate this clause.

Know Your Bill of Rights

Essay

Why do you think this clause is important in today's society? Do you agree with this clause? If not, explain.

The Sixth Amendment Key Words Drill

Purpose of this drill:

The purpose of this drill is to ensure you understand the basic words you will be coming across while studying the Sixth Amendment of the Bill of Rights.

How this drill is done:

This drill is done with another person. Both people are to read the drill's questions and answers before starting the drill.

The person asking the questions is the "coach," and the person answering is the "student." The coach asks the student the question, and the student answers it. The answer does not have to be word-for-word; just the concept must be correct.

If the student gets a question incorrect, the coach shows him or her the answer. The coach then has the student explain the answer in his or her own words. Once the student has it in his or her own words, the coach re-asks the question. The coach then continues with the next question. Once they've gone through all the questions, they start again from the beginning.

How to pass this drill:

The student is done with the drill when he or she can answer all the questions correctly, from the first to the last, without missing any.

The point of this drill is not for you to just memorize the answers to the questions, it is to help you actually understand the information.

Note:

Words often have several meanings. The definitions used in this drill only give the meaning that the word has as it is used in this workbook. To get the full understanding of each word, look at its other definitions in a dictionary.

QUESTIONS:

1. **What does *impartial* mean?**

   Having no direct involvement or interest and not favoring one person or side more than another.

2. **What does *ascertain* mean?**

   To find out something with certainty.

3. **What does *nature* mean?**

   The essential qualities of somebody or something.

4. **What does *compulsory* mean?**

   Required by law or an authority.

5. **What does *in one's favor* mean?**

   In a way that is good for you.

END OF DRILL

★ ★ ★

THE BILL OF RIGHTS
THE SIXTH AMENDMENT

In all criminal prosecutions, the accused shall enjoy the right to a speedy and public trial, by an impartial jury of the State and district wherein the crime shall have been committed, which district shall have been previously ascertained by law, and to be informed of the nature and cause of the accusation; to be confronted with the witnesses against him; to have compulsory process for obtaining witnesses in his favor, and to have the Assistance of Counsel for his defence.

Know Your Bill of Rights

Essay

Give your understanding of the following statement:

"In all criminal prosecutions, the accused shall enjoy the right to a speedy and public trial, by an impartial jury of the State and district wherein the crime shall have been committed, which district shall have been previously ascertained by law…"

Know Your Bill of Rights
Essay

Give three specific examples of freedoms or rights this clause gives you and others.

Know Your Bill of Rights Essay

Give three specific examples of restrictions this clause puts on the government.

Know Your Bill of Rights Essay

Give three specific examples of ways the government could violate this clause.

Know Your Bill of Rights

Essay

Why do you think this clause is important in today's society? Do you agree with this clause? If not, explain.

Know Your Bill of Rights

Essay

Give your understanding of the following statement:

"…and to be informed of the nature and cause of the accusation; to be confronted with the witnesses against him; to have compulsory process for obtaining witnesses in his favor, and to have the Assistance of Counsel for his defense."

Know Your Bill of Rights

Essay

Give three specific examples of freedoms or rights this clause gives you and others.

Know Your Bill of Rights

Essay

Give three specific examples of restrictions this clause puts on the government.

Know Your Bill of Rights Essay

Give three specific examples of ways the government could violate this clause.

Know Your Bill of Rights

Essay

Why do you think this clause is important in today's society? Do you agree with this clause? If not, explain.

The Seventh Amendment Key Words Drill

Purpose of this drill:

The purpose of this drill is to ensure you understand the basic words you will be coming across while studying the Seventh Amendment of the Bill of Rights.

How this drill is done:

This drill is done with another person. Both people are to read the drill's questions and answers before starting the drill.

The person asking the questions is the "coach," and the person answering is the "student." The coach asks the student the question, and the student answers it. The answer does not have to be word-for-word; just the concept must be correct.

If the student gets a question incorrect, the coach shows him or her the answer. The coach then has the student explain the answer in his or her own words. Once the student has it in his or her own words, the coach re-asks the question. The coach then continues with the next question. Once they've gone through all the questions, they start again from the beginning.

How to pass this drill:

The student is done with the drill when he or she can answer all the questions correctly, from the first to the last, without missing any.

The point of this drill is not for you to just memorize the answers to the questions, it is to help you actually understand the information.

Note:

Words often have several meanings. The definitions used in this drill only give the meaning that the word has as it is used in this workbook. To get the full understanding of each word, look at its other definitions in a dictionary.

QUESTIONS:

1. **What does *controversy* mean?**

   Disagreement or argument.

2. **What does *preserve* mean?**

   To defend, maintain or keep unimpaired.

3. **What does *otherwise* mean?**

   In any other ways.

4. **What is a *fact*?**

   An action; any thing done, or that comes to pass; an effect produced or achieved; an event.

5. **What does *according to* mean?**

   In agreement with.

END OF DRILL

★ ★ ★
The Bill of Rights
The Seventh Amendment

In suits at common law, where the value in controversy shall exceed twenty dollars, the right of trial by jury shall be preserved, and no fact tried by a jury, shall be otherwise re-examined in any Court of the United States, than according to the rules of the common law.

Know Your Bill of Rights Essay

Give your understanding of the following statement:

"In Suits at common law, where the value in controversy shall exceed twenty dollars, the right of trial by jury shall be preserved..."

Know Your Bill of Rights Essay

Give three specific examples of freedoms or rights this clause gives you and others.

Know Your Bill of Rights

Essay

Give three specific examples of ways the government could violate this clause.

Know Your Bill of Rights

Essay

Why do you think this clause is important in today's society? Do you agree with this clause? If not, explain.

Know Your Bill of Rights

Essay

Give your understanding of the following statement:

"...and no fact tried by a jury, shall be otherwise re-examined in any Court of the United States, than according to the rules of the common law."

The Eighth Amendment Key Words Drill

Purpose of this drill:

The purpose of this drill is to ensure you understand the basic words you will be coming across while studying the Eighth Amendment of the Bill of Rights.

How this drill is done:

This drill is done with another person. Both people are to read the drill's questions and answers before starting the drill.

The person asking the questions is the "coach," and the person answering is the "student." The coach asks the student the question, and the student answers it. The answer does not have to be word-for-word; just the concept must be correct.

If the student gets a question incorrect, the coach shows him or her the answer. The coach then has the student explain the answer in his or her own words. Once the student has it in his or her own words, the coach re-asks the question. The coach then continues with the next question. Once they've gone through all the questions, they start again from the beginning.

How to pass this drill:

The student is done with the drill when he or she can answer all the questions correctly, from the first to the last, without missing any.

The point of this drill is not for you to just memorize the answers to the questions, it is to help you actually understand the information.

Note:

Words often have several meanings. The definitions used in this drill only give the meaning that the word has as it is used in this workbook. To get the full understanding of each word, look at its other definitions in a dictionary.

QUESTIONS:

1. **What does *impose* mean?**

    To force something on someone such as a tax or a punishment.

2. **What does *cruel* mean?**

    Pleased to cause much pain or suffering to others, with no feelings of guilt.

3. **What does *inflict* mean?**

    To impose something unwelcome or painful on someone.

END OF DRILL

★ ★ ★

THE BILL OF RIGHTS
THE EIGHTH AMENDMENT

Excessive bail shall not be required, nor excessive fines imposed, nor cruel and unusual punishments inflicted.

The Story Behind The Eighth Amendment

> "I deem [one of] the essential principles of our government, and consequently [one] which ought to shape its administration…equal and exact justice to all men, of whatever state or persuasion, religious or political."
>
> – *Thomas Jefferson*

The Eighth Amendment was derived from a provision in the English Bill of Rights of 1689 that banned excessive bail. This prevented the once-frequent practice of judges fixing bail at impossibly high rates, leaving victims locked up indefinitely without trial. Parliament reformed that situation when it legislated that punishment should be proportionate to the severity of the crime.

The concept that punishment should not be vicious or inappropriately extreme but rather in proportion to the offense can be found in the Old Testament. Leviticus 24:19–20 says, "If a man injures his neighbor, what he has done must be done to him: broken limb for broken limb, eye for eye, tooth for tooth. As the injury inflicted, so much be the injury suffered." The Magna Carta later provided that "a freeman shall be amerced for a small offense only according to the degree of the offence; and for a grave offence he shall be amerced according to the gravity of the offence."

A fourteenth-century document took the policy on amercements and applied it to physical punishments, providing that punishment should be dealt "according to the nature and extent of the offence." In the mid-sixteenth century, Parliament granted that the kingdom would enjoy more security if the subjects loved their king and if laws did not impose severe penalties for misbehavior.

In 1583, Robert Beale denounced "the racking of grievous offenders, as being cruel, barbarous, contrary to law, and unto the liberty of English subjects." Beale was the first person to oppose torture even when sanctioned by the crown and one of the few Englishmen to object to "cruel" punishments. England had long forbade disproportionate or extreme punishments, but never "cruel" ones.

If a man committed a criminal offense, he could not be stripped of life, limb, or property unless first convicted by a jury, but he could not go to trial without his agreement. The court always asked whether an accused person would consent to trial by jury, and if he refused to plead, he would be subjected to "punishment strong and hard" until he permitted his trial. He was stripped, put in shackles in the worst part of the prison, fed only stale bread every other day, tortured by being prostrated, and then made to endure the slow pressing of as much iron as his body could bear, "and then more." The starvation, exposure, and pressing would continue until the victim either agreed to be tried or died.

Ironically, the torture was not designed to force a confession or self-incrimination; it was only to extort a plea, whether guilty or not guilty. In 1772, the law changed so that a prisoner who refused to answer an indictment of a felony should be treated as guilty, thus ending the extractions of pleas by torture. It was not until 1827 that a refusal to plead was entered as a plea of not guilty.

To better understand the history of criminal punishments, we should look to Sir William Blackstone's writings in his *Commentaries on the Law of England*. In it, he proudly touted the fact that the "humanity of the English nation has authorized, by tacit consent, an almost general mitigation of…torture or cruelty." English history, for example, showed few cases of disembowelment or immolation unless first deprived of sensation by strangulation. The usual physical punishments were exile, banishment, transportation, or imprisonment. England appropriated property; impaired rights to holding office, employment, and inheritance; and sometimes dismembered offenders by cutting off a hand or foot. It slit nostrils, branded, compelled hard labor, and used the pillory and ducking stool, but it did not break people's backs on the wheel, tie them to horses that ripped them apart, or bury them alive.

Blackstone felt the extreme punishments handed down during the reign of James II by the Court of the King's Bench were the catalyst for the provision in the English Bill of Rights that served as a model for the Eighth Amendment. Lord Chief Justice George Jeffreys, for example, sentenced 841 prisoners to be sent to the West Indies to live as slaves for not fewer than ten years. In one case, a young boy who criticized the government was convicted of seditious libel and sentenced to seven years' imprisonment and a flogging every other week through the towns of his shire—a punishment that was later reduced.

The English monarch could issue royal warrants authorizing the rack, which was frequently used. English law allowed such gruesome punishments as ripping out one's tongue, cutting off the nose or genitals, and, for capital crimes, boiling to death. The penalty for high treason was especially grisly: if male, he was hung but cut down before death, his genitals were then cut off and burned in front of him, he was then disemboweled and, while still alive, cut into four parts and beheaded. That punishment was outlawed in 1817, while quartering and beheading was prohibited in 1870. Women convicted of treason were strangled unconscious and then burned alive. This punishment ceased in 1790, while whipping them remained lawful until 1841.

The common punishments for lesser crimes were branding, nose slitting, and flogging. In 1630, a Puritan clergyman by the name of Alexander Leighton had libeled Anglican bishops and suffered a horrible retaliation: he was fined the staggering sum of ten thousand pounds (approximately three million in today's dollars), defrocked, whipped to the brink of death, pilloried with one ear nailed to the stocks that was then cut off, branded on his cheek, and had his nose slit. A week later, the same mutilations were carried out on the other side of his face, and he was then incarcerated for the rest of his life. Another Puritan martyr, William Prynne, had criticized theater plays that included women, though the queen occasionally acted on stage. He was pilloried, branded on his forehead, had his ears cut off, fined heavily, and sentenced to life in prison. Although the Star Chamber was abolished in 1641, excessively severe punishments endured.

The provision of the English Bill of Rights of 1689 against "cruel and unusual punishments" derived mainly from the reaction to the case of Titus Oates. Oates was an Anglican cleric who invented a hoax that the Catholics, led by Jesuit priests, intended to kill Charles II. Public hysteria followed, and at least fifteen people, including the Jesuit order's English leader, were disemboweled, quartered, and beheaded for high treason. When Oates's fabrication was discovered in 1685, he was indicted for perjury and sentenced to be defrocked, fined, whipped, imprisoned for life, and pilloried four times per year. Contemporaries considered his punishment cruel, even though severe whippings and life imprisonments were not unusual.

After the Revolution of 1689, Oates was released. He petitioned Parliament for redress, and while judges initially felt that his sentence was just because his perjuries resulted in the deaths of innocents, dissenting lords argued that a secular court could not defrock a clergyman and that harsh whippings and life in prison were "barbarous," "inhuman," "unchristian," and "unjust" punishments for perjury. The majority of the House of Lords agreed that "excessive bail ought not to be required nor excessive fines imposed, nor cruel nor unusual punishments inflicted." The House of Commons agreed, and as a result, the English Bill of Rights of 1689 outlawed cruel and unusual punishments.

The first American ban on cruel punishments appeared in the Massachusetts Body of Liberties of 1641, drafted by Nathaniel Ward of Ipswich. He declared that "for bodilie punishments we allow amongst us none that are inhumane Barbarous or cruell." Generally speaking, punishments in America were more lenient than in England. Robbers were branded and sometimes incarcerated for life. Mutilations were rare; women were hanged, not burned for witchcraft. Whipping was common, as were penalties such as the ducking stool and the pillory and penances such as the scarlet letter.

Six of the first thirteen states constitutionally banned cruel and unusual punishments, and a seventh did by statute. New Hampshire most fully detailed rights regarding punishment:

"All penalties ought to be proportioned to the nature of the offence. No wise legislature will affix the same punishment to the crimes of theft, forgery and the like, which they do to those of murder and treason; where the same undistinguishing severity is exerted against all offences; the people are led to forget the real distinction in the crimes themselves; and to commit the most flagrant with as little compunction as they do those of the lightest dye. For the same reason a multitude of sanguinary laws is both impolitic and unjust. The true design of all punishments being to reform; not to exterminate, mankind."

The Northwest Ordinance of 1787 provided a bill of rights that included a provision that read, "All fines shall be moderate, and no cruel or unusual punishments shall be inflicted." During the controversy over the ratification of the Constitution, the lack of protection against cruel and unusual punishments was decried by many. A Massachusetts delegate predicted that racks and gibbets "may be amongst the most mild instruments of their description." Patrick Henry and other Anti-Federalists proclaimed that Congress would order "tortures" and "barbarous punishments" as well as excessive fines.

When James Madison proposed the amendments that became the Bill of Rights, he again used the imperative verb "shall" when prohibiting cruel and unusual punishments instead of the weaker "ought." The Senate adopted Madison's wording verbatim.

The phrase "cruel and unusual punishment" referred to both the method and the severity of the penalty. Punishment had to be quick and as painless as possible and in no circumstances involve a lingering death or any type of torture. Death alone was acceptable punishment, so long as the victim had been provided due process of law and was convicted. As jurisprudence has taught us, an unusual punishment is constitutionally acceptable so long as it is not cruel. A new or unusual punishment that is administered swiftly and humanely is deemed within the bounds of constitutional law. But punishment must be weighed according to the offense, and no conventional form of punishment can be carried to the point where it becomes cruel.

Know Your Bill of Rights

Essay

Give your understanding of the following statement:

"Excessive bail shall not be required, nor excessive fines imposed, nor cruel and unusual punishments inflicted."

Know Your Bill of Rights

Essay

Give three specific examples of freedoms or rights this amendment gives you and others.

Know Your Bill of Rights

Essay

Give three specific examples of restrictions this amendment puts on the government.

Know Your Bill of Rights

Essay

Give three specific examples of ways the government could violate this amendment.

KNOW YOUR BILL OF RIGHTS

ESSAY

Why do you think this amendment is important in today's society? Do you agree with this amendment? If not, explain.

The Ninth Amendment Key Words Drill

Purpose of this drill:

The purpose of this drill is to ensure you understand the basic words you will be coming across while studying the Ninth Amendment of the Bill of Rights.

How this drill is done:

This drill is done with another person. Both people are to read the drill's questions and answers before starting the drill.

The person asking the questions is the "coach," and the person answering is the "student." The coach asks the student the question, and the student answers it. The answer does not have to be word-for-word; just the concept must be correct.

If the student gets a question incorrect, the coach shows him or her the answer. The coach then has the student explain the answer in his or her own words. Once the student has it in his or her own words, the coach re-asks the question. The coach then continues with the next question. Once they've gone through all the questions, they start again from the beginning.

How to pass this drill:

The student is done with the drill when he or she can answer all the questions correctly, from the first to the last, without missing any.

The point of this drill is not for you to just memorize the answers to the questions, it is to help you actually understand the information.

Note:

Words often have several meanings. The definitions used in this drill only give the meaning that the word has as it is used in this workbook. To get the full understanding of each word, look at its other definitions in a dictionary.

QUESTIONS:

1. **What is an *enumeration*?**

    The listing or naming of a number of things one by one.

2. **What does *construe* mean?**

    To understand the meaning of a word, phrase, gesture, etc. in a particular way.

3. **What does *disparage* mean?**

    To lower the opinion of; to degrade, injure or dishonor.

4. **What does *retain* mean?**

    To keep possession of something.

END OF DRILL

The Bill of Rights
The Ninth Amendment

The enumeration in the Constitution, of certain rights, shall not be construed to deny or disparage others retained by the people.

★ ★ ★

The Story Behind The Ninth Amendment

"Every government degenerates when trusted to the rulers of the people alone. The people themselves are its only safe depositories."

– *Thomas Jefferson*

The Ninth Amendment remained dormant for nearly 175 years, from 1791 to 1965, obscure in its meaning. In 1965, the Ninth Amendment was activated for the first time as grounds for declaring a government measure unconstitutional. Justice William O. Douglas, Associate Justice for the Supreme Court, confronted a state act that criminalized the use of contraceptives even for married couples when counseled by a physician.

Douglas called on the First, Third, Fourth, Fifth, and Ninth Amendments and declared a "right of privacy older than the Bill of Rights" with reference to the "sacred precincts of marital bedrooms." Three justices agreed that the Ninth Amendment supported the cancellation of such a state act.

Within fifteen years, the Ninth Amendment, inconspicuous for so long, was thrust into the limelight: it was invoked in more than twelve hundred state and federal cases of varied circumstances. Litigants found its utter lack of specificity as to rights protected irresistible, and everyone from schoolboys to police officers relied upon it, seeking to void regulations that governed length of hair, to require the regulation of the purity of water and air, and to claim a right to legal marriage between two people of the same sex.

But was the Ninth Amendment intended to be a fountain of unenumerated rights? Was it meant to simply be a receptacle for newly discovered rights embraced by activist judges? Like many other issues addressed in this workbook, there is much controversy over this question.

We can logically begin our analysis with the indisputable fact that the Ninth Amendment, by force of its terms, protects the unenumerated rights of the people: "The enumeration in the Constitution, of certain rights, shall not be construed to deny or disparage others retained by the people." This leads to the obvious question, what are those rights? The answer requires another question: Why did the Framers include an amendment that protects unenumerated rights when the government is granted no more authority to regulate the lives of citizens than what is precisely laid out in the Constitution?

For that answer, we need only to revisit the ratification controversy of the late 1700s. Ratificationists, including Framers, originally argued that a bill of rights was unnecessary because government derived all powers from the people and only possessed powers so delegated, and those powers could in no way be construed to include the authority to encroach on such rights.

The Federalist No. 84 argued that enumerating rights in the Constitution would not only be unnecessary, but even dangerous. The specious contention was that by protecting specific rights, it was implied that a governmental right to regulate such rights was in fact intended. Ratificationists also offered the weak argument that any explicit enumeration would never encompass all that could or should be protected, and by omitting rights from an enumeration, they might be presumed to be lost. Even James Madison, before he was the champion of the Bill of Rights, expressed similar concerns: "If an enumeration be made of all our rights, will it not be implied that everything omitted is given to the general government?"

Fortunately, such arguments were soundly defeated by the warning that despite the Constitution's apparent built-in protection of such rights, Congress might find ways to exercise its powers to abridge unenumerated rights. Additionally, the Federalist argument self-destructed through the simple irony that the Constitution, as originally ratified, explicitly protected certain rights, thus—per the Federalists' own warnings—exposing all those unenumerated rights to violation.

It did not take long for Madison to switch to the cause of adding amendments to the Constitution that would protect personal rights and thus erase the fears of many Anti-Federalists who were withholding support for the Constitution. Among Madison's proposals was one intended to guard against the possibility that unenumerated rights may be infringed: "The exceptions [to power] here or elsewhere in the constitution made in favor of particular rights, shall not be so construed as to diminish the just importance of other rights retained by the people, or as to enlarge the powers delegated by the constitution; but either as actual limitations on such powers, or as inserted merely for greater caution."

The Ninth Amendment was a conclusive solution to the problem of how to enumerate the people's rights without imperiling the many that are not described. The amendment was also a feasible way for Congress to avoid the laborious and likely controversial task of a complete enumeration as well as disarm any objections that the list of freedoms provided was incomplete.

The text of the Ninth Amendment clearly protects the unenumerated rights of the people, and no reason exists to believe that it means otherwise. What rights does the amendment protect, however? They had to be "natural rights" or "positive rights" according to Madison's great speech of June 8, wherein he lobbied for amendments. Freedom of speech, for example, is a natural right: one that preexisted government, inherent in human nature. The right to hold office and the right to free elections are examples of positive rights resulting from the social compact that creates government.

In 1775, Alexander Hamilton wrote that "the sacred rights of mankind are not to be rummaged for among old parchments or musty records. They are written, as with a sunbeam, in the whole volume of human nature, by the hand of the divinity itself, and can never be erased or obscured by mortal power." John Dickinson professed that such rights were claimed "from a higher source—from the King of kings, and Lord of all the earth. They are not annexed to us by parchments and seals. They are created in us by the decrees of Providence, which establish the laws of our nature. They are born with us; exist with us; and cannot be taken from us by any human power without taking our lives. In short, they are founded on the immutable maxims of reason and justice."

Let's also not forget the overarching theme of the new direction for America, as outlined in the Declaration of Independence: "We hold these truths to be self-evident, that all men are created equal; that they are endowed by their Creator with inherent and inalienable Rights; that among these, are Life, Liberty, and the pursuit of Happiness…"

The pursuit of happiness was a phrase John Locke commonly used in his writings on political ethics, and included in that concept were the great rights of liberty and property. This was not a radical concept. Sir William Blackstone remarked in his Commentaries in 1765 "that man should pursue his own happiness. This is the foundation of what we call ethics, or natural law."

The Framers wholeheartedly subscribed to Lockean thought, and "property" meant more than just material possessions. In his *Second Treatise of Government*, Locke wrote that people "united for the general preservation of their lives, liberties, and estates, which I call by the general name—property." He continued, "By property I must be understood here as in other places to mean that property which men have in their persons as well as goods." Locke used the word "property" to mean all that belongs to a person, especially his rights that he wished to retain. The founding generation of Americans understood this sense of the word, while modern citizens have lost it.

In an essay of 1792, Madison wrote that "property" embraces "every thing to which a man may attach a value and have a right." This included, of course, one's land, possessions, and money, but it also meant that "a man has property in his opinions and the free communication of them. He has a property of peculiar value in his religious opinions, and in the profession and practices dictated by them. He has property very dear to him in the safety and liberty of his person. He has an equal property in the free use of his faculties and free choice of the objects on which to employ them. In a word, as a man is said to have a right to his property, he may be equally said to have a property in his rights."

The Framers were not only deeply concerned about the protection of liberty, property, and the pursuit of happiness: they also believed in the principle that all people were born with an equality of rights and that all had a right to equal justice.

In short, the Ninth Amendment is the depository for our natural rights, including the right to pursue happiness and the right to equality of justice. Examples of such rights—rights fundamental to the pursuit of happiness—are the then-important right to hunt and fish, the right to travel, the right to intimate relations, and the right to privacy in matters of family and sex.

In addition to the protection of natural rights, the Ninth Amendment also secures our unenumerated positive rights, such as the right to not be taxed unless by consent of our chosen representatives, the right to be free from monopolies, the right of an accused person to be presumed innocent until proven guilty, and the right to have the prosecution bear the burden of proving a person's guilt beyond a reasonable doubt. Protection of these rights can be found in various state laws and constitutions and in the common law, and as such are rights of the people to which the power of government is subordinate.

The Ninth Amendment may have had the purpose of providing a haven for unknown rights that time would disclose. As the chief justice of Virginia's highest court pondered during the framing of the Bill of Rights, "May we not in the progress of things, discover some great and important [right], which we don't now think of?"

Regardless, this amendment has undoubtedly given the Constitution considerable flexibility to serve its purpose as society evolves, and it has empowered the courts to uphold the spirit of the Bill of Rights by remaining, as Madison put it, "the guardians of those rights; they will be an impenetrable bulwark against every assumption of power in the legislative or executive; they will be naturally led to resist every encroachment upon rights expressly stipulated for in the constitution by the declaration of rights."

As expected, the Ninth Amendment has also garnered more than its share of controversy, with courts continuing to discover new unenumerated rights and detractors howling against the rulings—whether the right to abortion, the right to privacy against electronic spying, or the right to dance in the nude.

The bottom line is that so long as we believe government's primary role is to secure the people's rights and must exercise all powers in subordination to them, the Ninth Amendment retains its intended vital function. The question is not whether the rights this amendment guarantees are as important as those clearly enumerated, but rather whether the courts should find certain unenumerated rights worthy of such protection and in line with the ideals on which our nation was founded.

Know Your Bill of Rights

Essay

Give your understanding of the following statement:

"The enumeration in the Constitution, of certain rights, shall not be construed to deny or disparage others retained by the people."

Know Your Bill of Rights Essay

Give three specific examples of freedoms or rights this amendment gives you and others.

Know Your Bill of Rights Essay

Give three specific examples of ways the government could violate this amendment.

Know Your Bill of Rights

Essay

Why do you think this amendment is important in today's society? Do you agree with this amendment? If not, explain.

The Tenth Amendment Key Words Drill

Purpose of this drill:

The purpose of this drill is to ensure you understand the basic words you will be coming across while studying the Tenth Amendment of the Bill of Rights

How this drill is done:

This drill is done with another person. Both people are to read the drill's questions and answers before starting the drill.

The person asking the questions is the "coach," and the person answering is the "student." The coach asks the student the question, and the student answers it. The answer does not have to be word-for-word; just the concept must be correct.

If the student gets a question incorrect, the coach shows him or her the answer. The coach then has the student explain the answer in his or her own words. Once the student has it in his or her own words, the coach re-asks the question. The coach then continues with the next question. Once they've gone through all the questions, they start again from the beginning.

How to pass this drill:

The student is done with the drill when he or she can answer all the questions correctly, from the first to the last, without missing any.

The point of this drill is not for you to just memorize the answers to the questions, it is to help you actually understand the information.

Note:

Words often have several meanings. The definitions used in this drill only give the meaning that the word has as it is used in this workbook. To get the full understanding of each word, look at its other definitions in a dictionary.

QUESTIONS:

1. **What does *delegate* mean?**

   To entrust to somebody else the power to act or make decisions.

2. **What does *reserve* mean?**

   To keep or hold; to retain.

3. **What does *respectively* mean?**

   Separately and individually and in the order already mentioned.

END OF DRILL

★ ★ ★

THE BILL OF RIGHTS
THE TENTH AMENDMENT

The powers not delegated to the United States by the Constitution, nor prohibited by it to the States, are reserved to the States respectively, or to the people.

Know Your Bill of Rights

Essay

Give your understanding of the following statement:

"**The powers not delegated to the United States by the Constitution, nor prohibited by it to the States, are reserved to the States respectively, or to the people.**"

Know Your Bill of Rights Essay

How does this amendment give freedoms or rights to the people?

Know Your Bill of Rights

Essay

How does this amendment put restrictions on the government or the people?

Know Your Bill of Rights
Essay

How does this amendment put restrictions on the government or the people?

Know Your Bill of Rights

Essay

How could the government violate this amendment?

Know Your Bill of Rights

Essay

Why do you think this amendment is important in today's society? Do you agree with this amendment? If not, explain.

Know Your Bill of Rights Essay

What freedoms granted by the Bill of Rights mean the most to you? Which do you feel most strongly about or enjoy the most?

Know Your Bill of Rights
Essay

Why do you think it is necessary to protect such freedoms with laws?

★ ★ ★

Your Greatest Defense

> "I know no safe depository of the ultimate powers of the society but the people themselves; and if we think them (the people) not enlightened enough to exercise their control with a wholesome discretion, the remedy is not to take it from them, but to inform their discretion by education. This is the true corrective of abuses of constitutional power."
>
> *– Thomas Jefferson*

First, I would like to congratulate you on completing this workbook. You now have a better understanding of your rights as an American than most citizens, and you will probably look at current political debates and trends in a much different light.

With your new understanding comes a new responsibility, however. Edmund Burke once wrote that "those who don't know history are destined to repeat it," and a cursory review of the trails of history going back to the earliest times reveals the bloody stains left by vicious oppressors who rose to absolute power.

Could you imagine being ruled by a lunatic who executed his own mother, burned Christian captives in his garden for light at night, and used treason laws to torture and kill anyone he considered a threat? The Romans suffered such a nightmare for fourteen years under the dominion of Emperor Nero (54–68).

What if your ruler had a penchant for skinning people alive, roasting them upon red-hot coals, and spoke of the "great beauty" of twitching bodies impaled on stakes? Such a despot existed: Vlad III, more commonly known as Vlad the Impaler, terrorized the region that is now Romania for six years (1456–1462).

How would you feel if your country were in the hands of a man who, through genocidal famines, mass executions, and forced labor camps, was responsible for the deaths of approximately twenty million victims? That is only a sampling from the annals of Joseph Stalin, who suppressed the Soviet Union for thirty-one years (1922–1953).

History has many, many other horrifying examples of tyrants using power to wantonly and sadistically repress populaces, but here is the point: while philosophers and theologians may argue whether Man is inherently evil, we can know that he is capable of evil deeds of stupefying magnitude and that he can execute his destructive plans with alarming brilliance and ambition. Indeed, some of the cruelest rulers in history were also some of the most intelligent and calculating, rising to power through ingenious intrigue and social and political maneuvering.

And what of the populations who allowed themselves to be subjected to such inhuman abuse? "The marvel of all history is the patience with which men and women submit to burdens unnecessarily laid upon them by their governments," wrote George Washington.

Now, you have to ask yourself a question: do you really think such tragedies could never happen again? Do you think that human nature has radically transformed and that somehow the "defects" that drove past dictators to such depths of depravity are magically gone? I think we can safely answer "no."

"Experience hath shown, that even under the best forms of government those entrusted with power have, in time, and by slow operations, perverted it into tyranny," said Thomas Jefferson.

How hard would it be for our country or civilization to regress into a form of domination familiar to our ancestors? To quote Burke again, "All that is necessary for the triumph of evil is that good men do nothing." Do not think that we are forever guaranteed the living conditions we inherited by some divine influence—history has thoroughly discredited that naïve assumption.

It took our species thousands of bloody, torturous, and degrading years to climb out of the pits of hell and recognize the sanctity of life, the value of the individual, and the equality of our fellows. To this effect, Madison proudly declared, "The happy Union of these States is a wonder; their Constitution a miracle; their example the hope of Liberty throughout the world." This is the legacy gifted to us by our ancestors; one that was purchased with the courage, blood, and lives of many millions.

Simply put, do you want the history books to remember you as a part of the hopeless derelicts who abandoned their rights and let their civilization sink back into a dark age of inequality and subjugation? Or do you want to be remembered like our ancestors, to whom this workbook was dedicated? Brave, tough-minded patriots who sounded the alarm against the dangers of government oppression of the individual and who risked their lives and fortunes to uphold their beliefs that government is but an instrument of the people, its powers forever subordinate to their rights as human beings.

If you were concerned enough to finish this workbook, then I am sure I can count you among the latter. The greatest human victories have not been million-strong armies led by sociopathic demagogues, smashing cities to pieces and slaughtering and enslaving their fellow Man over religion, politics, territory, or even pettier disputes. The greatest human victories have been the milestones of Man's ascent from barbarism and superstition to civility and enlightenment, and these were accomplished through the steel will and courage of individuals with the audacity to defy what surely appeared as insurmountable juggernauts possessed of unlimited power.

As technology marches forward, would-be oppressors have more options than ever to enslave us in ways that our Founders would have never imagined. If only the tyrants of the past had today's mind-altering pharmaceuticals to turn their subjects into unfeeling, unthinking automatons incapable of even comprehending the world around them, let alone caring enough to effect actual change in it. If only they had the technology to track, record, and even predict every aspect of our lives with which they could weed out dissenters and undesirables.

So, what can we do, then?

"Educate and inform the whole mass of the people…they are the only sure reliance for the preservation of our liberty," wrote Jefferson.

You are your first line of defense, along with your friends, family, co-workers, association members, and community. They must understand their rights and feel as adamant about them as you now do. So please give them this workbook and see that they complete it. Promote it to everyone you know and fortify our safeguard one person at a time, thus protecting yourself and everyone you care about.

And beware of sophists who try to dismiss your natural rights as passé or antiquated. Cultures change, societies evolve, and our lives become more and more sophisticated, but time and the trappings of our modern existence can never strip us of our humanity and our freedom to, as Blackstone said, pursue our own happiness. When that is lost, nothing else matters.

People who would attempt to violate, diminish, or eliminate your rights as taught in this workbook are, in effect, trying to degrade your value as a human being. They are trying to covertly assert their superiority over you and get you to believe that, as Orwell said, slavery is freedom.

You have already taken the first step to resisting such horror, and all you have to do is continue one foot at a time and invite others to join you.

Madison boldly declared that governments are instituted for the sole reason of securing the people "in the enjoyment of life and liberty, with the right of acquiring and using property, and generally of pursuing and obtaining happiness and safety."

Let's together do what it takes to provide that great truth with the vitality it needs to see us and our descendants through the centuries to come.

The Know Your Bill of Rights Workbook

Appendix

The United States Bill of Rights

Preamble

Congress OF THE United States

begun and held at the City of New York, on Wednesday

the Fourth of March, one thousand seven hundred and eighty nine.

THE Conventions of a number of the States having at the time of their adopting the Constitution, expressed a desire, in order to prevent misconstruction or abuse of its powers, that further declaratory and restrictive clauses should be added: And as extending the ground of public confidence in the Government, will best insure the beneficent ends of its institution

RESOLVED by the Senate and House of Representatives of the United States of America, in Congress assembled, two thirds of both Houses concurring, that the following Articles be proposed to the Legislatures of the several States, as Amendments to the Constitution of the United States, all or any of which Articles, when ratified by three fourths of the said Legislatures, to be valid to all intents and purposes, as part of the said Constitution; viz.:

ARTICLES in addition to, and Amendment of the Constitution of the United States of America, proposed by Congress, and ratified by the Legislatures of the several States, pursuant to the fifth Article of the original Constitution.

Amendment I

Congress shall make no law respecting an establishment of religion, or prohibiting the free exercise thereof; or abridging the freedom of speech, or of the press; or the right of the people peaceably to assemble, and to petition the Government for a redress of grievances.

Amendment II

A well regulated Militia, being necessary to the security of a free State, the right of the people to keep and bear Arms, shall not be infringed.

Amendment III

No Soldier shall, in time of peace be quartered in any house, without the consent of the

Owner, nor in time of war, but in a manner to be prescribed by law.

Amendment IV

The right of the people to be secure in their persons, houses, papers, and effects, against unreasonable searches and seizures, shall not be violated, and no Warrants shall issue, but upon probable cause, supported by Oath or affirmation, and particularly describing the place to be searched, and the persons or things to be seized.

Amendment V

No person shall be held to answer for a capital, or otherwise infamous crime, unless on a presentment or indictment of a Grand Jury, except in cases arising in the land or naval forces, or in the Militia, when in actual service in time of War or public danger; nor shall any person be subject for the same offence to be twice put in jeopardy of life or limb; nor shall be compelled in any criminal case to be a witness against himself, nor be deprived of life, liberty, or property, without due process of law; nor shall private property be taken for public use, without just compensation.

Amendment VI

In all criminal prosecutions, the accused shall enjoy the right to a speedy and public trial, by an impartial jury of the State and district wherein the crime shall have been committed, which district shall have been previously ascertained by law, and to be informed of the nature and cause of the accusation; to be confronted with the witnesses against him; to have compulsory process for obtaining witnesses in his favor, and to have the Assistance of Counsel for his defence.

Amendment VII

In suits at common law, where the value in controversy shall exceed twenty dollars, the right of trial by jury shall be preserved, and no fact tried by a jury, shall be otherwise reexamined in any Court of the United States, than according to the rules of the common law.

Amendment VIII

Excessive bail shall not be required, nor excessive fines imposed, nor cruel and unusual punishments inflicted.

Amendment IX

The enumeration in the Constitution, of certain rights, shall not be construed to deny or disparage others retained by the people.

Amendment X

The powers not delegated to the United States by the Constitution, nor prohibited by it to the States, are reserved to the States respectively, or to the people.

THE UNITED STATES CONSTITUTION

We the People of the United States, in Order to form a more perfect Union, establish Justice, insure domestic Tranquility, provide for the common defence, promote the general Welfare, and secure the Blessings of Liberty to ourselves and our Posterity, do ordain and establish this Constitution for the United States of America.

Article. I.

Section. 1.

All legislative Powers herein granted shall be vested in a Congress of the United States, which shall consist of a Senate and House of Representatives.

Section. 2.

The House of Representatives shall be composed of Members chosen every second Year by the People of the several States, and the Electors in each State shall have the Qualifications requisite for Electors of the most numerous Branch of the State Legislature.

No Person shall be a Representative who shall not have attained to the Age of twenty five Years, and been seven Years a Citizen of the United States, and who shall not, when elected, be an Inhabitant of that State in which he shall be chosen.

Representatives and direct Taxes shall be apportioned among the several States which may be included within this Union, according to their respective Numbers, which shall be determined by adding to the whole Number of free Persons, including those bound to Service for a Term of Years, and excluding Indians not taxed, three fifths of all other Persons. The actual Enumeration shall be made within three Years after the first Meeting of the Congress of the United States, and within every subsequent Term of ten Years, in such Manner as they shall by Law direct. The Number of Representatives shall not exceed one for every thirty Thousand, but each State shall have at Least one Representative; and until such enumeration shall be made, the State of New Hampshire shall be entitled to chuse three, Massachusetts eight, Rhode-Island and Providence Plantations one, Connecticut five, New-York six, New Jersey four, Pennsylvania eight, Delaware one, Maryland six, Virginia ten, North Carolina five, South Carolina five, and Georgia three.

When vacancies happen in the Representation from any State, the Executive Authority thereof shall issue Writs of Election to fill such Vacancies.

The House of Representatives shall chuse their Speaker and other Officers; and shall have the sole Power of Impeachment.

Section. 3.

The Senate of the United States shall be composed of two Senators from each State, chosen by the Legislature thereof for six Years; and each Senator shall have one Vote.

Immediately after they shall be assembled in Consequence of the first Election, they shall be divided as equally as may be into three Classes. The Seats of the Senators of the first Class shall be vacated at the Expiration of the second Year, of the second Class at the Expiration of the fourth Year, and of the third Class at the Expiration of the sixth Year, so that one third may be chosen every second Year; and if Vacancies happen by Resignation, or otherwise, during the Recess of the Legislature of any State, the Executive thereof may make temporary Appointments until the next Meeting of the Legislature, which shall then fill such Vacancies.

No Person shall be a Senator who shall not have attained to the Age of thirty Years, and been nine Years a Citizen of the United States, and who shall not, when elected, be an Inhabitant of that State for which he shall be chosen.

The Vice President of the United States shall be President of the Senate, but shall have no Vote, unless they be equally divided.

The Senate shall chuse their other Officers, and also a President pro tempore, in the Absence of the Vice President, or when he shall exercise the Office of President of the United States.

The Senate shall have the sole Power to try all Impeachments. When sitting for that Purpose, they shall be on Oath or Affirmation. When the President of the United States is tried, the Chief Justice shall preside: And no Person shall be convicted without the Concurrence of two thirds of the Members present.

Judgment in Cases of Impeachment shall not extend further than to removal from Office, and disqualification to hold and enjoy any Office of honor, Trust or Profit under the United States: but the Party convicted shall nevertheless be liable and subject to Indictment, Trial, Judgment and Punishment, according to Law.

Section. 4.

The Times, Places and Manner of holding Elections for Senators and Representatives, shall be prescribed in each State by the Legislature thereof; but the Congress may at any time by Law make or alter such Regulations, except as to the Places of chusing Senators.

The Congress shall assemble at least once in every Year, and such Meeting shall be on the first Monday in December, unless they shall by Law appoint a different Day.

Section. 5.

Each House shall be the Judge of the Elections, Returns and Qualifications of its own

Members, and a Majority of each shall constitute a Quorum to do Business; but a smaller Number may adjourn from day to day, and may be authorized to compel the Attendance of absent Members, in such Manner, and under such Penalties as each House may provide.

Each House may determine the Rules of its Proceedings, punish its Members for disorderly Behaviour, and, with the Concurrence of two thirds, expel a Member.

Each House shall keep a Journal of its Proceedings, and from time to time publish the same, excepting such Parts as may in their Judgment require Secrecy; and the Yeas and Nays of the Members of either House on any question shall, at the Desire of one fifth of those Present, be entered on the Journal.

Neither House, during the Session of Congress, shall, without the Consent of the other, adjourn for more than three days, nor to any other Place than that in which the two Houses shall be sitting.

Section. 6.

The Senators and Representatives shall receive a Compensation for their Services, to be ascertained by Law, and paid out of the Treasury of the United States. They shall in all Cases, except Treason, Felony and Breach of the Peace, be privileged from Arrest during their Attendance at the Session of their respective Houses, and in going to and returning from the same; and for any Speech or Debate in either House, they shall not be questioned in any other Place.

No Senator or Representative shall, during the Time for which he was elected, be appointed to any civil Office under the Authority of the United States, which shall have been created, or the Emoluments whereof shall have been encreased during such time; and no Person holding any Office under the United States, shall be a Member of either House during his Continuance in Office.

Section. 7.

All Bills for raising Revenue shall originate in the House of Representatives; but the Senate may propose or concur with Amendments as on other Bills.

Every Bill which shall have passed the House of Representatives and the Senate, shall, before it become a Law, be presented to the President of the United States: If he approve he shall sign it, but if not he shall return it, with his Objections to that House in which it shall have originated, who shall enter the Objections at large on their Journal, and proceed to reconsider it. If after such Reconsideration two thirds of that House shall agree to pass the Bill, it shall be sent, together with the Objections, to the other House, by which it shall likewise be reconsidered, and if approved by two thirds of that House, it shall become a Law. But in all such Cases the Votes of both Houses shall be determined by yeas and Nays, and the Names of the Persons voting for and against the Bill shall be entered on the Journal of each House respectively. If any Bill shall not be returned by the President within ten Days (Sundays excepted) after it shall have been presented to him, the Same shall be a Law, in like Manner as if he had signed it, unless the Congress by their Adjournment prevent its Return, in which Case it shall not be a Law.

Every Order, Resolution, or Vote to which the Concurrence of the Senate and House of Representatives may be necessary (except on a question of Adjournment) shall be presented to the President of the United States; and before the Same shall take Effect, shall be approved by him, or being disapproved by him, shall be repassed by two thirds of the Senate and House of Representatives, according to the Rules and Limitations prescribed in the Case of a Bill.

Section. 8.

The Congress shall have Power To lay and collect Taxes, Duties, Imposts and Excises, to pay the Debts and provide for the common Defence and general Welfare of the United States; but all Duties, Imposts and Excises shall be uniform throughout the United States;

To borrow Money on the credit of the United States;

To regulate Commerce with foreign Nations, and among the several States, and with the Indian Tribes;

To establish an uniform Rule of Naturalization, and uniform Laws on the subject of Bankruptcies throughout the United States;

To coin Money, regulate the Value thereof, and of foreign Coin, and fix the Standard of Weights and Measures;

To provide for the Punishment of counterfeiting the Securities and current Coin of the United States;

To establish Post Offices and post Roads;

To promote the Progress of Science and useful Arts, by securing for limited Times to Authors and Inventors the exclusive Right to their respective Writings and Discoveries;

To constitute Tribunals inferior to the supreme Court;

To define and punish Piracies and Felonies committed on the high Seas, and Offences against the Law of Nations;

To declare War, grant Letters of Marque and Reprisal, and make Rules concerning Captures on Land and Water;

To raise and support Armies, but no Appropriation of Money to that Use shall be for a longer Term than two Years;

To provide and maintain a Navy;

To make Rules for the Government and Regulation of the land and naval Forces;

To provide for calling forth the Militia to execute the Laws of the Union, suppress Insurrections and repel Invasions;

To provide for organizing, arming, and disciplining, the Militia, and for governing such Part of them as may be employed in the Service of the United States, reserving to the States respectively, the Appointment of the Officers, and the Authority of training the Militia according to the discipline prescribed by Congress;

To exercise exclusive Legislation in all Cases whatsoever, over such District (not exceeding ten Miles square) as may, by Cession of particular States, and the Acceptance of Congress, become the Seat of the Government of the United States, and to exercise like Authority over all Places purchased by the Consent of the Legislature of the State in which the Same shall be, for the Erection of Forts, Magazines, Arsenals, dock-Yards, and other needful Buildings;--And

To make all Laws which shall be necessary and proper for carrying into Execution the foregoing Powers, and all other Powers vested by this Constitution in the Government of the United States, or in any Department or Officer thereof.

Section. 9.

The Migration or Importation of such Persons as any of the States now existing shall think proper to admit, shall not be prohibited by the Congress prior to the Year one thousand eight hundred and eight, but a Tax or duty may be imposed on such Importation, not exceeding ten dollars for each Person.

The Privilege of the Writ of Habeas Corpus shall not be suspended, unless when in Cases of Rebellion or Invasion the public Safety may require it.

No Bill of Attainder or ex post facto Law shall be passed.

No Capitation, or other direct, Tax shall be laid, unless in Proportion to the Census or enumeration herein before directed to be taken.

No Tax or Duty shall be laid on Articles exported from any State.

No Preference shall be given by any Regulation of Commerce or Revenue to the Ports of one State over those of another; nor shall Vessels bound to, or from, one State, be obliged to enter, clear, or pay Duties in another.

No Money shall be drawn from the Treasury, but in Consequence of Appropriations made by Law; and a regular Statement and Account of the Receipts and Expenditures of all public Money shall be published from time to time.

No Title of Nobility shall be granted by the United States: And no Person holding any Office of Profit or Trust under them, shall, without the Consent of the Congress, accept of any present, Emolument, Office, or Title, of any kind whatever, from any King, Prince, or foreign State.

Section. 10.

No State shall enter into any Treaty, Alliance, or Confederation; grant Letters of Marque and Reprisal; coin Money; emit Bills of Credit; make any Thing but gold and silver Coin a Tender in

Payment of Debts; pass any Bill of Attainder, ex post facto Law, or Law impairing the Obligation of Contracts, or grant any Title of Nobility.

No State shall, without the Consent of the Congress, lay any Imposts or Duties on Imports or Exports, except what may be absolutely necessary for executing it's inspection Laws: and the net Produce of all Duties and Imposts, laid by any State on Imports or Exports, shall be for the Use of the Treasury of the United States; and all such Laws shall be subject to the Revision and Controul of the Congress.

No State shall, without the Consent of Congress, lay any Duty of Tonnage, keep Troops, or Ships of War in time of Peace, enter into any Agreement or Compact with another State, or with a foreign Power, or engage in War, unless actually invaded, or in such imminent Danger as will not admit of delay.

Article. II.

Section. 1.

The executive Power shall be vested in a President of the United States of America. He shall hold his Office during the Term of four Years, and, together with the Vice President, chosen for the same Term, be elected, as follows:

Each State shall appoint, in such Manner as the Legislature thereof may direct, a Number of Electors, equal to the whole Number of Senators and Representatives to which the State may be entitled in the Congress: but no Senator or Representative, or Person holding an Office of Trust or Profit under the United States, shall be appointed an Elector.

The Electors shall meet in their respective States, and vote by Ballot for two Persons, of whom one at least shall not be an Inhabitant of the same State with themselves. And they shall make a List of all the Persons voted for, and of the Number of Votes for each; which List they shall sign and certify, and transmit sealed to the Seat of the Government of the United States, directed to the President of the Senate. The President of the Senate shall, in the Presence of the Senate and House of Representatives, open all the Certificates, and the Votes shall then be counted. The Person having the greatest Number of Votes shall be the President, if such Number be a Majority of the whole Number of Electors appointed; and if there be more than one who have such Majority, and have an equal Number of Votes, then the House of Representatives shall immediately chuse by Ballot one of them for President; and if no Person have a Majority, then from the five highest on the List the said House shall in like Manner chuse the President. But in chusing the President, the Votes shall be taken by States, the Representation from each State having one Vote; A quorum for this purpose shall consist of a Member or Members from two thirds of the States, and a Majority of all the States shall be necessary to a Choice. In every Case, after the Choice of the President, the Person having the greatest Number of Votes of the Electors shall be the Vice President. But if there should remain two or more who have equal Votes, the Senate shall chuse from them by Ballot the Vice President.

The Congress may determine the Time of chusing the Electors, and the Day on which they shall give their Votes; which Day shall be the same throughout the United States.

No Person except a natural born Citizen, or a Citizen of the United States, at the time of the Adoption of this Constitution, shall be eligible to the Office of President; neither shall any Person be eligible to that Office who shall not have attained to the Age of thirty five Years, and been fourteen Years a Resident within the United States.

In Case of the Removal of the President from Office, or of his Death, Resignation, or Inability to discharge the Powers and Duties of the said Office, the Same shall devolve on the Vice President, and the Congress may by Law provide for the Case of Removal, Death, Resignation or Inability, both of the President and Vice President, declaring what Officer shall then act as President, and such Officer shall act accordingly, until the Disability be removed, or a President shall be elected.

The President shall, at stated Times, receive for his Services, a Compensation, which shall neither be increased nor diminished during the Period for which he shall have been elected, and he shall not receive within that Period any other Emolument from the United States, or any of them.

Before he enter on the Execution of his Office, he shall take the following Oath or Affirmation:- -"I do solemnly swear (or affirm) that I will faithfully execute the Office of President of the United States, and will to the best of my Ability, preserve, protect and defend the Constitution of the United States."

Section. 2.

The President shall be Commander in Chief of the Army and Navy of the United States, and of the Militia of the several States, when called into the actual Service of the United States; he may require the Opinion, in writing, of the principal Officer in each of the executive Departments, upon any Subject relating to the Duties of their respective Offices, and he shall have Power to grant Reprieves and Pardons for Offences against the United States, except in Cases of Impeachment.

He shall have Power, by and with the Advice and Consent of the Senate, to make Treaties, provided two thirds of the Senators present concur; and he shall nominate, and by and with the Advice and Consent of the Senate, shall appoint Ambassadors, other public Ministers and Consuls, Judges of the supreme Court, and all other Officers of the United States, whose Appointments are not herein otherwise provided for, and which shall be established by Law: but the Congress may by Law vest the Appointment of such inferior Officers, as they think proper, in the President alone, in the Courts of Law, or in the Heads of Departments.

The President shall have Power to fill up all Vacancies that may happen during the Recess of the Senate, by granting Commissions which shall expire at the End of their next Session.

Section. 3.

He shall from time to time give to the Congress Information of the State of the Union, and recommend to their Consideration such Measures as he shall judge necessary and expedient; he may, on extraordinary Occasions, convene both Houses, or either of them, and in Case of Disagreement between them, with Respect to the Time of Adjournment, he may adjourn them to such Time as he shall think proper; he shall receive Ambassadors and other public Ministers; he shall take Care that the Laws be faithfully executed, and shall Commission all the Officers of the United States.

Section. 4.

The President, Vice President and all civil Officers of the United States, shall be removed from Office on Impeachment for, and Conviction of, Treason, Bribery, or other high Crimes and Misdemeanors.

Article III.

Section. 1.

The judicial Power of the United States shall be vested in one supreme Court, and in such inferior Courts as the Congress may from time to time ordain and establish. The Judges, both of the supreme and inferior Courts, shall hold their Offices during good Behaviour, and shall, at stated Times, receive for their Services a Compensation, which shall not be diminished during their Continuance in Office.

Section. 2.

The judicial Power shall extend to all Cases, in Law and Equity, arising under this Constitution, the Laws of the United States, and Treaties made, or which shall be made, under their Authority;-- to all Cases affecting Ambassadors, other public Ministers and Consuls;--to all Cases of admiralty and maritime Jurisdiction;--to Controversies to which the United States shall be a Party;--to Controversies between two or more States;-- between a State and Citizens of another State,-- between Citizens of different States,--between Citizens of the same State claiming Lands under Grants of different States, and between a State, or the Citizens thereof, and foreign States, Citizens or Subjects.

In all Cases affecting Ambassadors, other public Ministers and Consuls, and those in which a State shall be Party, the supreme Court shall have original Jurisdiction. In all the other Cases before mentioned, the supreme Court shall have appellate Jurisdiction, both as to Law and Fact, with such Exceptions, and under such Regulations as the Congress shall make.

The Trial of all Crimes, except in Cases of Impeachment, shall be by Jury; and such Trial shall be held in the State where the said Crimes shall have been committed; but when not committed within any State, the Trial shall be at such Place or Places as the Congress may by Law have directed.

Section. 3.

Treason against the United States, shall consist only in levying War against them, or in adhering to their Enemies, giving them Aid and Comfort. No Person shall be convicted of Treason unless on the Testimony of two Witnesses to the same overt Act, or on Confession in open Court.

The Congress shall have Power to declare the Punishment of Treason, but no Attainder of Treason shall work Corruption of Blood, or Forfeiture except during the Life of the Person attainted.

Article. IV.

Section. 1.

Full Faith and Credit shall be given in each State to the public Acts, Records, and judicial Proceedings of every other State. And the Congress may by general Laws prescribe the Manner in which such Acts, Records and Proceedings shall be proved, and the Effect thereof.

Section. 2.

The Citizens of each State shall be entitled to all Privileges and Immunities of Citizens in the several States.

A Person charged in any State with Treason, Felony, or other Crime, who shall flee from Justice, and be found in another State, shall on Demand of the executive Authority of the State from which he fled, be delivered up, to be removed to the State having Jurisdiction of the Crime.

No Person held to Service or Labour in one State, under the Laws thereof, escaping into another, shall, in Consequence of any Law or Regulation therein, be discharged from such Service or Labour, but shall be delivered up on Claim of the Party to whom such Service or Labour may be due.

Section. 3.

New States may be admitted by the Congress into this Union; but no new State shall be formed or erected within the Jurisdiction of any other State; nor any State be formed by the Junction of two or more States, or Parts of States, without the Consent of the Legislatures of the States concerned as well as of the Congress.

The Congress shall have Power to dispose of and make all needful Rules and Regulations respecting the Territory or other Property belonging to the United States; and nothing in this Constitution shall be so construed as to Prejudice any Claims of the United States, or of any particular State.

Section. 4.

The United States shall guarantee to every State in this Union a Republican Form of Government, and shall protect each of them against Invasion; and on Application of the Legislature, or of the Executive (when the Legislature cannot be convened), against domestic Violence.

Article. V.

The Congress, whenever two thirds of both Houses shall deem it necessary, shall propose Amendments to this Constitution, or, on the Application of the Legislatures of two thirds of the several States, shall call a Convention for proposing Amendments, which, in either Case, shall be valid to all Intents and Purposes, as Part of this Constitution, when ratified by the Legislatures of three fourths of the several States, or by Conventions in three fourths thereof, as the one or the other Mode of Ratification may be proposed by the Congress; Provided that no Amendment which may be made prior to the Year One thousand eight hundred and eight shall in any Manner affect the first and fourth Clauses in the Ninth Section of the first Article; and that no State, without its Consent, shall be deprived of its equal Suffrage in the Senate.

Article. VI.

All Debts contracted and Engagements entered into, before the Adoption of this Constitution, shall be as valid against the United States under this Constitution, as under the Confederation.

This Constitution, and the Laws of the United States which shall be made in Pursuance thereof; and all Treaties made, or which shall be made, under the Authority of the United States, shall be the supreme Law of the Land; and the Judges in every State shall be bound thereby, any Thing in the Constitution or Laws of any State to the Contrary notwithstanding.

The Senators and Representatives before mentioned, and the Members of the several State Legislatures, and all executive and judicial Officers, both of the United States and of the several States, shall be bound by Oath or Affirmation, to support this Constitution; but no religious Test shall ever be required as a Qualification to any Office or public Trust under the United States.

Article. VII.

The Ratification of the Conventions of nine States, shall be sufficient for the Establishment of this Constitution between the States so ratifying the Same.

The Word, "the," being interlined between the seventh and eighth Lines of the first Page, the Word "Thirty" being partly written on an Erazure in the fifteenth Line of the first Page, The Words "is tried" being interlined between the thirty second and thirty third Lines of the first Page and the Word "the" being interlined between the forty third and forty fourth Lines of the second Page.

Attest William Jackson Secretary

done in Convention by the Unanimous Consent of the States present the Seventeenth Day of September in the Year of our Lord one thousand seven hundred and Eighty seven and of the Independance of the United States of America the Twelfth In witness whereof We have hereunto subscribed our Names,

G°. Washington
Presidt. and deputy from Virginia

Delaware
Geo: Read
Gunning Bedford jun
John Dickinson
Richard Bassett
Jaco: Broom

Maryland
James McHenry
Dan of St Thos. Jenifer
Danl. Carroll

Virginia
John Blair
James Madison Jr.

North Carolina
Wm. Blount
Richd. Dobbs Spaight
Hu Williamson

South Carolina
J. Rutledge

Charles Cotesworth Pinckney
Charles Pinckney
Pierce Butler

Georgia
William Few
Abr Baldwin

New Hampshire
John Langdon
Nicholas Gilman

Massachusetts
Nathaniel Gorham
Rufus King

Connecticut
Wm. Saml. Johnson
Roger Sherman

New York
Alexander Hamilton

New Jersey
Wil: Livingston
David Brearley

Wm. Paterson

Jona: Dayton

Pennsylvania

B Franklin

Thomas Mifflin

Robt. Morris

Geo. Clymer

Thos. FitzSimons

Jared Ingersoll

James Wilson

Gouv Morris

Glossary

abridge: to reduce or lessen in duration, extent or range, authority, etc.; to diminish.

abuse: wrong or improper use.

according: in agreement with.

accusation: a claim that somebody has done something illegal or wrong.

acquittal: formal certification by the court of the innocence of a person charged with a crime. Ordinarily this occurs after a trial by a finding of "not guilty" by a judge or jury. An acquittal may also take place before trial because the charges are improper or there isn't enough evidence.

Acton, Lord: a British historian of the late nineteenth and early twentieth centuries.

admonish: to advise to do or against doing something; caution.

adversarial system: in the adversarial system, two or more opposing parties gather evidence and present the evidence and their arguments to a judge or jury. The judge or jury knows nothing of the lawsuit until the parties present their cases to the decision maker.

affirmation: a formal declaration, acceptable in court, given in place of a sworn statement by a person who conscientiously objects to taking an oath.

affix: to attach, unite, or connect with.

afford: to make available; provide.

amendment: 1. a word, clause or paragraph, added or proposed to be added to a bill before a legislature. **2.** an article added to the U.S. Constitution.

amerce: to punish with an arbitrary penalty.

Anglican: relating to or indicating the Church of England or any Church in connection with it.

Anglicanism: the faith of the Anglican Church, the group of Christian churches historically based in the Church of England. Anglicans combine Catholic and Protestant elements in their teaching, worship, and government. They have bishops, for example, but don't accept the authority of the Pope. The word *Anglican* originates in *ecclesia anglicana*, a medieval Latin phrase dating to at least 1246 meaning *the English Church*. Followers of Anglicanism are called *Anglicans*.

annal: a record of events year by year.

Anti-Federalism: Anti-Federalism refers to a movement that opposed the strong central government envisioned in the Constitution of the United States of 1787. While admitting the need for changes in the Articles of Confederation, Anti-Federalists feared that a strong federal government would infringe on states' rights. Led by Patrick Henry of Virginia, Anti-Federalists worried, among other things, that the position of president, then something new, might evolve into a monarchy.

appropriate: take for one's own use without permission.

arbitrary: 1. based on personal wishes, feelings, or perceptions, rather than on fixed rules. **2.** based on the decision of a judge or court rather than in accordance with any rule or law.

Articles of Confederation: the document that set forth the terms under which the original thirteen states agreed to participate in a centralized form of government, in addition to their self-rule, and that was in effect from 1781 to 1789, prior to the adoption of the Constitution.

article: a clause or paragraph of a legal document or agreement, typically one outlining a single rule or law.

Article 5 of the U.S. Constitution: the fifth article of the U.S. Constitution details the procedure of how Congress can propose and ratify amendments to the Constitution.

Articles of Confederation: an agreement among the thirteen original states, approved in 1781, that provided a loose federal government before the present Constitution went into effect in 1789.

ascertain: find out something with certainty.

ascribe: to attribute something to (as a cause).

assemble: to gather together for a common purpose.

assistance of counsel: assistance of counsel means that the criminal defendant has had a competent attorney representing him or her.

Associate Justice: any U.S. Supreme Court Justice, other than the Chief Justice.

Atlantis: a legendary island, beautiful and prosperous, which was said to have been swallowed up in an earthquake and now covered by the sea.

attainder, bill of: an act of legislature finding a person guilty of treason or felony without trial.

Attorney General: the head of the Department of Justice and a member of the President's Cabinet. He serves as legal advisor to the President and to all agencies of the executive branch and is the chief law-enforcement officer of the United States Government. The office of Attorney General is one of the most powerful in government. His opinions on legal matters have the force of law unless overturned by a court.

audacity: the willingness to take bold risks.

augment: to make greater, more numerous, larger, or more intense.

authority: 1. legal power or a right to command or to act. 2. a person or group of persons that are given the power to command or control, especially to enforce the law.

automaton: a moving mechanical device made in imitation of a human being.

badge: a mark, sign, or thing, by which a person or thing is distinguished.

bail: a sum of money given to a court to secure an accused person's temporary release from arrest and to guarantee the person will appear in court at a later date. If the person fails to appear in court on the date set, the money is lost.

banishment: the state of being sent away, especially from a country, as an official punishment.

baron: a British nobleman of the lowest rank.

barrister: in Great Britain, a lawyer who may argue cases in superior courts.

bayonet: a detachable, daggerlike blade put on the end of a rifle, for hand-to-hand fighting.

Beale, Robert: (1541–1601) an English diplomat and administrator during Elizabeth I's reign. As Clerk of the Privy Council, Beale wrote the official record of the execution of Mary, Queen of Scots, to which he was an eyewitness.

beneficent: showing active goodness or causing good to be done; producing benefits or advantages.

bill of attainder: an act of legislature finding a person guilty of treason or felony without trial.

bill: a draft of a proposed law presented to a legislature, but not yet passed and made law.

Blackstone, Sir William: (1723–1780) an English expert and writer on law noted particularly for his *Commentaries on the Laws of England (1765–69)*, which had a great influence on jurisprudence in the U.S.

body: a group of people united by their jobs or activities.

brand: to burn a distinctive mark into or upon with a hot iron, to indicate quality, ownership, etc., or to mark as infamous (as a convict).

bulwark: that which secures against an enemy or external annoyance; a screen or shelter; means of protection and safety.

Burgh, James: (1714–1775) an English Whig who made a significant contribution to free speech. Many of his other writings contributed in other areas such as educational reform.

but (upon): *but* in this usage means *except* and *upon* means *at the time of*. If you were to say no checks will be written but upon an authorized purchase order, you mean that nobody will receive a check unless they can give an authorized purchase order.

but: only.

canon law: the law governing the affairs of a Christian Church, especially the law created or recognized by those in the Roman Catholic Church. The church courts had very wide jurisdiction—for example, in England, control of the law of personal property—and because they were well regulated, they tended to attract many borderline cases that might also have been heard by the developing royal courts

capital: involving or bringing about punishment by death.

capricious: given to sudden and unaccountable changes of mood or behavior.

cardinal: of the greatest importance; fundamental.

case: a matter examined or judged in a court of law.

catalyst: a person or thing acting as the stimulus in bringing about or hastening a result.

cause: a reason for an action or response.

caveat: a modifying or cautionary detail to be considered when evaluating, interpreting, or doing something.

censorship: the suppression of all or a part of something considered offensive or unacceptable.

census: a numbering of the people, and valuation of their estate, for the purpose of imposing taxes, etc., usually made once every five or ten years.

Chancellor of the Exchequer: the finance minister of the United Kingdom, responsible for preparing the nation's budget.

charge: make an accusation or assertion that.

checks and balances: a fundamental principle of American government, guaranteed by the Constitution, where each branch of the government (executive, judicial, legislative) has some amount of influence over the other branches and may choose to block procedures of the other branches. Checks and balances prevent any one branch from accumulating too much power and encourages cooperation between branches.

cherish: to take good care of; protect.

Chief Justice: the highest judicial officer of the United States or of a state. The Chief Justice of the United States is appointed for a life term by the President with the consent of the Senate. In the states, the chief justices are elected for a limited term. Aside from administrative duties and a slightly higher salary, chief justices have no more power than other members of highest courts in deciding cases. The position, however, does carry considerable prestige.

civil law: one of the two major legal systems of the modern Western world (the other is *common law*). In this system, a highly structured and rigid code of rules is followed exactly, and an expert judge decides cases without the help of a jury. Under this system, every defendant who enters a criminal trial is presumed guilty until proven innocent, whereas under common law (practiced in most English-speaking countries) he or she is presumed innocent until proven guilty. Louisiana is the only state in the U.S. whose law is based entirely on civil law. However, remnants of civil law remain in other states (as Texas and California) in which countries of continental Europe had a strong influence.

clause: a part of a contract, agreement, will, or other writing.

clergy: the body of all people ordained for religious duties, especially in a Christian Church.

clergyman: a priest or minister of a Christian church.

cleric: a priest or religious leader, especially a Christian or Muslim one.

clerk: an official responsible (as to a government agency) for correspondence, records, and accounts and vested with specified powers or authority.

cliché: a phrase or opinion that is overused and betrays a lack of original thought.

Coke, Sir Edmund: (1552–1634) an English expert on law and Member of Parliament whose writings on the common law were the authoritative legal texts for nearly 150 years.

commentary: a brief account of transactions or events written hastily, as if for a memorandum—usually in the plural.

common law: one of the two major legal systems of the modern Western world (the other is civil law), it originated in the UK and is now followed in most English-speaking countries. Initially, common law was founded on common sense as reflected in the social customs. Over the centuries, it was replaced by statute law (rules enacted by a legislative body such as a Parliament) and clarified by the judgments of the higher courts (that set a precedent for all courts to follow in similar cases). Under civil law, every defendant who enters a criminal trial is presumed guilty until proven innocent, whereas under common law he or she is presumed innocent until proven guilty.

common sense: good judgment based on a simple understanding of the facts, not on special knowledge or training.

compact: a formal agreement or contract between two or more parties.

compel: to drive, urge or force by physical, legal, social or moral means.

compensation: an amount of money or something else given to pay for loss, damage or work done.

compulsory: that must be done, undergone, etc.; required.

compunction: the pain of sorrow or regret of having violated a moral duty; strong feeling of uneasiness caused by guilt.

concur: to agree.

Congress: the legislative body of the United States, composed of the Senate and the House of Representatives. **NOTE:** For a bill to be passed and made law, it must be approved by a majority vote in both the House and the Senate, and then must be approved by the President. If the President rejects a bill, the Senate and House can override him with a two-thirds vote in favor, and the bill becomes law. Additionally, the Senate and House have different exclusive powers. For example, only the Senate can approve treaties (agreements to international laws), while only the House can initiate spending bills and move to impeach people holding governmental positions.

conscience: internal or self-knowledge, or judgment of right and wrong; the sense or power within us, warning against and condemning that which is wrong, and approving and prompting that which is right; the moral sense.

consent: acceptance of or agreement to something proposed or desired by another.

constitution: 1. a document that outlines the basic laws, rules, and principles by which a country or organization is governed. **2.** U.S. Constitution. A document that embodies the fundamental laws and principles by which the United States is governed. It was drafted by the Constitutional Convention in 1787 and later supplemented by the Bill of Rights and other amendments. See also *Constitutional Convention*.

Constitutional Convention: the gathering that drafted the Constitution of the United States in 1787; all states were invited to send delegates. The convention, meeting in Philadelphia, designed a government with separate legislative, executive, and judicial branches. It established Congress as a lawmaking body with two houses: each state is given two representatives in the Senate, whereas representation in the House of Representatives is based on population.

construe: to understand the meaning of a word, phrase, gesture, etc. in a particular way.

contemptuous: feeling, expressing, or demonstrating a strong dislike or utter lack of respect for somebody or something.

controversy: disagreement or argument.

convention: a meeting or formal gathering of people for the discussion of and action on particular matters of public concern (things that involve and affect many people).

counsel: a lawyer or group of lawyers who conduct cases in court or give legal advice.

Court of High Commission: was the supreme ecclesiastic court in England. It became a controversial force of control, used against those who refused to acknowledge the authority of the Church of England. Its main function, and the most controversial, was administration of the oath *ex officio*, committing one to answer even self-incriminating questions; those who refused to take the oath were turned over to the feared Court of Star Chamber. Opposition, mainly from the Puritans and the common lawyers, resulted in the court's abolishment by Parliament in 1641.

court of law: a place where legal cases are heard and decided, especially in front of a judge and jury.

Court of Star Chamber: a royal court existing in England from the 15th century until 1641. The court was set up to ensure the fair enforcement of laws against prominent people, those so powerful that ordinary courts could never convict them of their crimes. Court sessions were held in secret, with no indictments, no right of appeal, no juries, and no witnesses. Evidence was presented in writing. Over time it evolved into a political weapon, a symbol of the misuse and abuse of power by the English monarchy and courts. The name came from the courtroom's ceiling, which was painted with stars.

criminal case: a lawsuit brought by an attorney employed by the government that charges a person with the commission of a crime.

cruel and unusual punishment: a phrase describing governmental penalties against convicted criminals which are barbaric, involve torture and/or shock the public morality. They are specifically prohibited under the Eighth Amendment to the U.S. Constitution.

cruel: pleased to cause much pain or suffering to others, with no feelings of guilt.

Cuddihy, William J.: the author of *The Fourth Amendment: Origins and Original Meaning 602 – 1791*, a book on the historical background of the Fourth Amendment.

cudgel: a short, thick stick used as a weapon.

cull: select from a large quantity; obtain from a variety of sources.

cursory: going rapidly over something, without noticing details; hasty.

customs: 1. the official department that administers and collects the taxes imposed by a government on imported goods. **2.** duties or taxes imposed on imported and, less commonly, exported goods.

Dark Ages: the period of European history between the fall of the Roman Empire in 476 A.D. and about 1000 A.D. Though sometimes taken to derive its meaning from the fact that little was then known about the period, the term's more usual and negative sense is of a period of intellectual darkness and absence of culture.

debar: to hinder from approach, entry or enjoyment; to shut out or exclude.

declaration: the act of making known by words or by other means.

declaratory: stating and clarifying something, especially a legal right, status, order, or judgment.

decree: in religion, the predetermined purpose of God, whose plan of operations is unchangeable.

decry: to speak out against strongly and openly.

deem: to think; to judge; to be of opinion.

defrock: to deprive of the rank or function of priest or minister.

delegate: to entrust to somebody else the power to act or make decisions.

Delaware Declaration of Rights: the Delaware Constitution of 1776. It was the first governing document for Delaware's state government.

demagogue: a leader who makes use of popular prejudices and false claims and promises in order to gain power.

demagoguery: the methods and practices of a *demagogue*, a leader who makes use of popular prejudices and false claims and promises in order to gain power.

demark: *demarcate*; to separate clearly as if by boundaries; distinguish.

Dennis vs. United States: a United States Supreme Court case involving Eugene Dennis, general secretary of the Communist Party USA, which found that Dennis did not have a right under the First Amendment to the Constitution to exercise free speech, publication, and assembly, if that exercise advanced a conspiracy to overthrow the government.

denomination: a group or branch of any religion.

denounce: publicly declare to be wrong or evil.

Department of Justice: a major department of the federal executive branch, headed by the Attorney General, which administers the Federal Bureau of Investigation, prosecutes violations of federal law, and is responsible for enforcing all civil rights laws.

deposition: the act of giving testimony under oath.

depository: a place where things are put for safekeeping.

deprive: to take something away from somebody.

despotic: of or like a despot, a ruler or other person who holds absolute power, typically one who exercises it in a cruel way.

detractor: a person who criticizes someone or something.

Dick, Philip K.: (1928–1982) an American novelist, short story writer, and essayist whose published work is almost entirely in the science fiction genre.

Dickson, John: (1732–1808) an American lawyer and politician who represented both Delaware and Pennsylvania. He voted against and declined to sign the Declaration of Independence, but then served in the American Revolutionary militia. As a member of the Constitutional Convention, he supported ratification of the Constitution. His numerous political writings earned him the title of "Penman of the Revolution."

Digest: a *digest* is a compilation of rules of law based on decided cases. *The Digest* is an arrangement of excerpts from the writings and opinions of distinguished lawyers, contained in fifty books compiled by order of Emperor Justinian in the sixth century.

disarm: 1. to deprive of arms (weapons), usually by force or authority. **2.** lessen the hostility or suspicions of.

disembowel: cut open and remove the internal organs of.

dismember: to remove the limbs by cutting or tearing.

disparage: to lower the opinion of; to degrade, injure or dishonor.

dissent: (used with *from*) to disagree in opinion; to differ; to think in a different or contrary manner.

dissident: a person who disagrees with an established religious or political system, organization, or belief.

district: one of the territorial areas into which an entire state or country, county, city, or other political subdivision is divided, for judicial, political, electoral, or administrative purposes.

divergent: tending to be different or develop in different directions.

Double Jeopardy: the act of prosecuting a defendant a second time for an offense for which he has already been tried.

Douglas, William Orville: (1898–1980) an Associate Justice of the United States Supreme Court. With a term lasting 36 years and 209 days, he is the longest-serving justice in the history of the Supreme Court. He established the records for the most opinions written, the most objections written, the most speeches given, and the most books authored by any member of the Supreme Court.

draconian: (of laws or their application) excessively harsh and severe.

draft: a first form of any writing, which may be changed.

ducking stool: a chair or stool used for the punishment of offenders by plunging them into water.

due process of law: the administration of justice according to established rules and principles; based on the principle that a person cannot be deprived of life or liberty or property without appropriate legal procedures and safeguards

due: meeting all the necessary requirements and thus proper and appropriate to the situation.

duty: a tax on goods, especially imports or exports.

dye, of the lightest: variation of *the deepest dye*, which means of the most extreme or the worst sort. Of *the lightest dye* then means that which is not extreme or terrible.

dystopian: an imagined place or state in which everything is unpleasant or bad, typically a totalitarian or environmentally degraded one; the opposite of *utopian*.

ecclesiastical law: the body of laws and regulations made or adopted by ecclesiastical authority, for the government of the Christian organization and its members.

ecclesiastical: of or pertaining to the Christian church; relating to the organization or government of the Church; not secular.

effects: somebody's personal possessions or the things that somebody is carrying on him or her.

elect: to select by vote.

Ellsworth, Oliver: (1745–1807) an American lawyer and politician, a revolutionary against British rule, a drafter of the United States Constitution, and the third Chief Justice of the United States.

embitter: make (someone) feel bitter or resentful.

embodiment: a tangible or visible form of an idea, quality, or feeling.

Emerson, Ralph Waldo: (1803–1882) an American writer and philosopher. His poems, orations, and especially his essays, such as Nature (1836), are regarded as landmarks in the development of American thought and literary expression.

enactment: that which is passed into a law.

end: the reason why something exists or why action is taken; the purpose or goal.

English Civil War: also known as the Great Rebellion (1642–1651), conflict in England between King Charles I and Parliament. A parliamentary victory resulted in the King's execution, the exile of his heir, Charles II, and the establishment of a Commonwealth under Oliver Cromwell. The war is sometimes called the Puritan Revolution because most of the King's opponents belonged to the Puritan party in the Church of England.

enlist: to enroll for service in some branch of the armed forces.

entrench: to place in a position of strength; establish firmly or solidly.

enumeration: the listing or naming of a number of things one by one.

epitomize: to shorten, abridge, or give a summary of (a written work).

equity: a branch of law that provides a remedy where the common law does not apply. The common law is concerned largely with granting damages after a wrongful action. Equity is designed to provide justice where damages may come too late to be meaningful. In an equity case, the court may order that something be done or forbid certain actions. Equity procedures are less formal than regular court procedures, and juries are seldom used.

established: in place and generally recognized as being true or valid.

establishment: the recognition of a church by law as the official church of a nation or state and supported by civil authority.

Ex officio: a Latin term meaning by virtue of one's position or status. Many hold a position on a board or agency by virtue of their holding some other related position. For example, the Vice President serves ex officio as president of the Senate.

ex post facto: a descriptive term for an explanation or a law that is made up after an event and then applied to it. *Ex post facto* is Latin for "from after the deed."

exact: 1. demand and obtain from someone. 2. inflict (revenge) on someone.

excise: an internal tax imposed on the production, sale, or consumption of a commodity or the use of a service within a country.

executive branch: the branch of federal and state government that is broadly responsible for implementing, supporting, and enforcing the laws made by the legislative branch and interpreted by the judicial branch. At the state level, the executive includes governors and their staffs. At the federal level, the executive includes the president, vice president, staffs of appointed advisers (including the cabinet), and a variety of departments and agencies, such as the Central Intelligence Agency (CIA), the Federal Bureau of Investigation (FBI), and the Postal Service.

exercise: to put something into action or use.

exile: to force (someone) to leave his or her own country, community, etc.; banish.

extend (or gain) ground: to gain approval or acceptance. **NOTE:** *Ground*, in this context, means "the foundation that supports any thing."

extort: obtain by force, threats, or other unfair means.

fact: an action; any thing done, or that comes to pass; an effect produced or achieved; an event.

favor, in one's: in a way that is good for oneself.

federal: 1. of or relating to a form of government or a country in which power is divided between one central and several regional governments. 2. pertaining to the national government level, as opposed to state, provincial, county, city, or town.

feudal: 1. absurdly outdated or old-fashioned. 2. according to, resembling, or having to do with the system of *feudalism*, the social system that developed in western Europe in the eighth and ninth centuries in which people served a man of high rank by working and fighting for him and in exchange were supported and given land and protection.

Federalist No. 84: an essay by Alexander Hamilton, part of "Federalist Papers," a series of 85 essays written by Alexander Hamilton, James Madison and John Jay, which were published in New York newspapers in 1787 to convince New Yorkers to adopt the newly proposed Constitution drafted in Philadelphia.

fine: a sum of money that somebody is ordered to pay for breaking a law or rule.

firelock: a musket, or other gun, with a lock, which is discharged by striking fire with flint and steel.

flagpole: a pole on which a flag is raised and flown.

flint: a massive hard dark quartz that produces a spark when struck by steel.

flog: to beat with a strap, stick, whip, etc.

formal: done in a way that follows the established rules.

Founding Father: a general name for male American patriots during the Revolutionary War, especially the signers of the Declaration of Independence and those who drafted the Constitution. John Adams, Benjamin Franklin, Alexander Hamilton, Thomas Jefferson, James Madison, and George Washington were all Founding Fathers.

frame: to shape, create, or form, usually according to a pattern; design.

freedom of the press: the right to publish and distribute broadly information, thoughts and opinions without restraint or censorship.

freedom: the ability to act, speak or think as one wants without resistance or restraint.

frontier: the extreme limit of understanding or achievement in a particular area.

garner: to collect or gather.

gibbet: an upright post with an arm on which the bodies of executed criminals were left hanging as a warning or deterrent to others.

Gilbert, Chief Baron Geoffrey: (1674–1726) an English judge and author who was Lord Chief Baron of the Exchequer in both Ireland and England and later became renowned for his legal treatises, none of which were published in his lifetime.

Glorious Revolution: (also known as the *Bloodless Revolution*) in British history, the events surrounding the removal of James II from the throne and his replacement in 1689 by his daughter Mary and William of Orange as joint sovereigns. James II had become increasingly unpopular on account of his unconstitutional behavior and Catholicism. The Glorious Revolution was bloodless in England, but involved fierce wars in both Scotland and Ireland.

govern: to direct and control, either by established laws or individual judgments.

government: the group of persons who direct the actions of societies and states according to the established constitution and laws or by arbitrary decisions.

grand jury: a group of 12 to 23 jurors responsible for deciding whether someone accused of a crime should be brought to trial in a court of law.

grievance: a wrong considered as a valid reason for complaint, or something believed to cause pain, worry, sorrow, etc.

grievous: **1.** unreasonably burdensome or severe. **2.** hurtful; destructive; causing mischief.

grill: to question intensely.

grisly: causing a shudder or feeling of horror; horrible; gruesome.

habeas corpus: a legal term meaning that an accused person must be presented physically before the court with a statement demonstrating sufficient cause for arrest. Thus, no accuser may imprison someone indefinitely without bringing that person and the charges against him or her into a courtroom. In Latin, *habeas corpus* literally means "you shall have the body."

Hale, Sir Matthew: (1609–1676) an influential English lawyer, judge, and expert on law.

Hamilton, Alexander: (1755–1804) a Founding Father, soldier, economist, political philosopher, one of America's first constitutional lawyers and the first United States Secretary of Treasury.

hamstrung: severely restricted of efficiency or effectiveness.

Hawkins, William: (1673–1746) a barrister and Serjeant-at-Law, best known for his work on the English criminal law, *Treatise of Pleas of the Crown.*

held to answer: being held by the police or other authorities to go to trial for supposedly committing a crime. Example sentence: The man was arrested and held to answer on murder charges.

Henry Lee, Richard: (1732–1794) an American statesman from Virginia best known for the motion in the Second Continental Congress calling for the colonies' independence from Great Britain. His famous resolution of June 1776 led to the United States Declaration of Independence, which Lee signed. As U.S. Senator from Virginia, Lee was largely responsible for adoption of the first 10 amendments (the Bill of Rights) to the Constitution.

Henry, Patrick: a political leader of the eighteenth century, known for his fiery oratory. He is especially remembered for saying, "Give me liberty or give me death."

heresy: any opinion (in philosophy, politics, religion, etc.) opposed to official or established views or doctrines.

House of Commons: in British history the House of Commons was the representatives of the people, in contrast to the nobles. Today it is the lower house of the parliament of Britain. It includes representatives from England, Northern Ireland, Scotland, and Wales, all elected by the people.

House of Representatives: one of the two elected legislative bodies of the United States, composed of 435 members with 6 additional members who can't vote. (One non-voting delegate is chosen from each: Puerto Rico, The District of Columbia, and the territories of American Samoa, Guam, the Northern Mariana Islands, and the U.S. Virgin Islands. These delegates cannot vote, but can participate in debates.) **NOTE:** The number of representatives for each state is determined by the population of the states (larger population means more representatives in the House).

house: a legislative group in a government, or the place where they meet.

hue and cry: any loud public outcry.

illustrious: notably or brilliantly outstanding because of dignity or achievements or actions.

immolate: kill or offer as a sacrifice, especially by burning.

immunity: freedom or exemption from any charge, duty, obligation, office, tax, penalty, or service.

immutable: unchanging over time or unable to be changed.

impair: weaken or damage.

impartial: having no direct involvement or interest and not favoring one person or side more than another.

imperative: indicating the mood of a verb that expresses a command or strong request.

impolitic: failing to possess or display good sense; unwise.

impose: to force something on someone such as a tax or punishment.

impost: a tax or similar required payment.

impressment: the act of pressing or forcing someone into any service.

inalienable: that may not be taken away, surrendered, or transferred.

independent: free from the authority, control or rule of somebody or something else.

indict: to charge with the commission of a crime, especially to make a formal accusation against on the basis of positive legal evidence—usually said of the action of a grand jury.

indictment: a formal written accusation charging one or more persons with the commission of a crime, presented by a grand jury to the court when the jury has found, after examining the evidence presented, that there is a valid case. A document called a *bill of indictment* used to be signed by the grand jury to finalize the accusation (but it's now signed by a court official).

infamous: 1. well known for some bad quality or deed. 2. punishable by severe measures, such as death, long imprisonment, or loss of rights.

infamy: extremely bad reputation, public reproach, or strong condemnation as the result of a shameful, criminal, or outrageous act.

inference: a conclusion reached on the basis of evidence and reasoning.

inflict: to impose something unwelcome or painful on someone.

infringe: 1. to break; to violate; to neglect to fulfill or obey. 2. to limit or reduce someone's legal rights or freedom, whether by intervention or not fulfilling some duty.

inquisitorial: pertaining to a trial with one person or group inquiring into the facts and acting as both prosecutor and judge. In the inquisitorial system, the presiding judge is primarily responsible for supervising the gathering of the evidence necessary to resolve the case. He or she actively steers the search for evidence and questions the witnesses, including the respondent or defendant.

inscribe: write or carve (words or symbols) on something, especially as a formal or permanent record.

insidious: operating or proceeding in an inconspicuous or seemingly harmless way but actually with grave effect.

institution: establishment; that which is appointed, agreed, or founded by authority, and intended to be permanent. The word *institution* is applied to laws, rites, and ceremonies, which are ordered by authority as permanent rules of conduct or of government.

insurrection: an act or instance of rising in revolt, rebellion, or resistance against civil authority or an established government.

interlineation: the act of inserting words or lines between lines before written or printed.

inviolable: not capable of being broken or violated.

inviolate: free or safe from injury or violation; unbroken.

invoke: appeal to (someone or something) as an authority for an action or in support of an argument.

Ipswich: a town of eastern England near the North Sea northeast of London.

James II and VII: (1633–1701) King of England and King of Ireland as James II and King of Scotland as James VII, in 1685. As a Roman Catholic, he was unpopular because he tried to force Protestant England to become Catholic. He was forced to give up his rule in 1688, during the Glorious Revolution, after which William III became king with his wife, Mary II. James died, exiled in France, in 1701.

Jefferson, Thomas: (1743–1826) the third president of the United States and one of the drafters of the Declaration of Independence. Besides serving two terms as president (from 1801 to 1809), Jefferson served as vice-president, secretary of state, minister to France, congressman, and governor of Virginia. Jefferson is best remembered as a champion of human rights and the lead draftsman of the Declaration of Independence. The third person to be president, Jefferson followed John Adams as president and was succeeded by James Madison.

Jeffreys, George: (1645–1689), also known as "The Hanging Judge," was England's most hated judge. Jeffreys took wicked pleasure in torturing those who appeared before him. In 1688 when James II fled the country, Jeffreys was placed in the Tower of London for his own safety. He died there the following year of kidney disease.

jeopardy: 1. the risk of loss, harm, death or destruction. **2.** danger arising from being on trial for a criminal offense.

Jesuit: a member of the Roman Catholic Society of Jesus founded by St. Ignatius Loyola in 1534 and devoted to missionary and educational work.

Johnson, Zachariah: a delegate to the Virginia Ratifying Convention in 1788.

judicature: the action of judging; the administration of justice.

Judiciary Act of 1789: a law passed by the first Congress to establish the federal court system. The Act determined the organization and jurisdiction of the courts. Over the years, the Judiciary Act has undergone numerous changes, adding and deleting courts, changing jurisdiction of courts, and establishing rules of procedure.

juggernaut: a huge, powerful, and overwhelming force or institution.

jurisprudence: the science or art of law.

jury: a group of people, usually twelve, chosen to give a decision on a legal case that is presented before them in a court of law.

just: right or fair.

Justinian I, Emperor: the Emperor Justinian I ruled the Eastern Roman, or Byzantine, Empire from 527 until 565. He is noteworthy for his efforts to regain the lost provinces of the Western Roman Empire, his Codification of Roman Law, and his architectural achievements.

keep: to hold; to continue to have something and not lose or part with it.

King James Bible: the best-known English Translation of the Bible, commissioned by King James I of England and published in the early seventeenth century. It is also known as the Authorized Version. In the late nineteenth century, the Revised Version was published in England.

King's Bench: formerly, the highest court of common law in England—so called because the king used to sit there in person.

laborious: involving or calling for much hard work; difficult.

larceny: the unlawful taking and removing of another's personal property with the intent of permanently depriving the owner; theft.

law: 1. a system of rules that a particular country or community recognizes as regulating the actions of its members and may enforce by the use of penalties.

2. a rule of conduct or procedure as a part of such a system, enforceable by an authority.

legal: provided or permitted by the law.

legislate: to make or pass a law or laws.

legislative: involved in the writing and passing of laws.

legislature: 1. a group of persons, usually elected, that have the authority to make, change and cancel laws. **2.** the branch of government having the power to make laws, as distinguished from the executive and judicial branches of government. In the U.S., as laid down by the Constitution, only Congress can make laws. Congress is composed of the Senate (100 members, 2 per state) and House of Representative (435 members plus 6 who can't vote), usually chosen by election, with the power to make, change, and cancel laws.

lest: with the intention of preventing (something undesirable); to avoid the risk of.

Leveller: the Levellers were an informal alliance of agitators and pamphleteers who came together during the English Civil War (1642-1648) to demand constitutional reform and equal rights under the law. Levellers believed all men were born free and equal and possessed natural rights that resided in the individual, not the government. "Leveller" was a term of abuse, coined by their opponents to exaggerate the threat of their ideas.

Leviticus: the third book of the Bible, containing laws relating to the priests and Levites (priests of the tribe of Levi) and to the forms of Jewish ceremonies.

lexicographer: one who writes, compiles, or edits a dictionary.

libel: 1. a written, printed, or pictorial statement that unjustly defames someone publicly. **2.** to damage the reputation of someone, or expose to public hatred, contempt, or ridicule, by a writing, picture, sign, etc.

liberalize: remove or loosen restrictions on something, usually an economic or political system.

libertarian: somebody who believes in the principle that people should have complete freedom of thought and action.

liberty: freedom from restraint or control regarding one's body, actions or mind.

life or limb: when talking of criminal punishments, "life or limb" was used to refer to those involving the actual loss of natural life or limb. **NOTE:** The words "life or limb" are currently not interpreted strictly in the legal application of the 5th Amendment; they are used to refer to any criminal penalty. This may or may not have been the intention of the Framers.

Lilburne, John: (1614-1657), also known as Freeborn John, was an English political advocate for the abolition of the monarchy before, during and after English Civil Wars 1642-1650. He coined the term "freeborn rights," defining them as rights with which every human is born, as opposed to rights given by government or law.

litigant: a person involved in a lawsuit.

Livermore, Samuel: (1732-1803) a U.S. politician. He was a U.S. Senator from New Hampshire from 1793 to 1801.

lobby: to attempt to influence a public official in favor of something (often with for).

Locke, John: (1632-1704) a philosopher who argued against the belief that human beings are born with certain ideas already in their minds. He claimed that, on the contrary, the mind is a blank slate until experience begins to "write" on it. In his political writings, Locke attacked the doctrine of the divine right of kings and argued that governments depend on the consent of the governed. Locke's political ideas were taken up by the Founding Fathers; his influence is especially apparent in the Declaration of Independence.

Long Parliament: the name commonly given to the English Parliament that sat from November 1640 to March 1653, was restored for a short time in 1659, and finally voted its own end in 1660. During this period King Charles I was put to death and England was declared a commonwealth. The earlier Short Parliament, which met for three weeks in 1640, had been dominated by the king. The Long Parliament, on the other hand, was the real ruling power of England until the rise of Oliver Cromwell in the 1650s. Never again was the monarchy to dominate Parliament.

luminary: a person who inspires or influences others.

Madison, James: (1751–1836) an American politician and political philosopher who served as the fourth President of the United States (1809–1817) and is one of the Founding Fathers of the United States. He was the principal author of the U.S. Constitution, and is often called the "Father of the Constitution."

magistrate: a person with authority to administer the law or one possessing large judicial or executive authority. In this broad sense the word is used in such phrases as "the first magistrate" of a king in a monarchy or "the chief magistrate" of the president of the United States.

Magna Carta: a list of rights and privileges that King John of England signed under pressure from English noblemen in 1215. It established the principles that the king could not demand taxes without consent of his legislature, or parliament, and that no free man in England could be deprived of liberty and property except through a trial or other legal process.

manner: the way in which something is done or happens.

Mason, George: (1725–1792) was an American patriot, statesman, and a delegate from Virginia to the U.S. Constitutional Convention. Along with James Madison, he is called the "Father of the Bill of Rights," and is one of the Founding Fathers of the United States.

Massachusetts Body of Liberties of 1641: was the first legal code established by European colonists in New England. It incorporates rights that were later judged to be ahead of their time, with some of these rights eventually appearing in the Bill of Rights.

Massachusetts Declaration of Rights: the 1780 Constitution of the Commonwealth of Massachusetts, drafted by John Adams, is the world's oldest functioning written constitution. It served as a model for the United States Constitution.

matrix: something that constitutes the place or point from which something else originates, takes form, or develops.

maxim: an established principle or proposition; a principle generally received or admitted as true.

mea culpa: used as an acknowledgment of one's fault or error. For example, "I gave you the wrong directions to my house—mea culpa." From Latin, meaning "by my fault."

misconstruction: an act of misunderstanding the meaning of. Example sentence: His misconstruction of my statement led to an upset.

mitigate: make less severe, serious, or painful.

mockery: words or behavior intended to make something or somebody look silly or ridiculous.

moral sense: the ability to determine the rightness or wrongness of actions.

moreover: in addition to what has been said; besides; further; also.

musket: a long-barreled firearm, used especially by foot soldiers before the invention of the rifle.

nation: a body of people inhabiting the same country, or united under the same sovereign or government; as the English nation or the French nation.

nature: the essential qualities of somebody or something.

New Hampshire Declaration of Rights: the Constitution of the State of New Hampshire. It is the primary governing document of the State of New Hampshire. The constitution became effective June 2, 1784, when it replaced the state's constitution of 1776.

nor: and not.

Northwest Ordinance: a law passed in 1787 that established a government for the Northwest Territory, outlined the process for admitting a new state to the Union, and guaranteed that newly created states would be equal to the original thirteen states. Considered one of the most important legislative acts of the Confederation Congress, the Northwest

Ordinance also protected civil liberties and outlawed slavery in the new territories.

notwithstanding: nevertheless; however; although.

Oates, Titus: (1649–1705) an English conspirator who fabricated the "Popish Plot," a supposed Catholic conspiracy to kill King Charles II.

oath: a formal and legally binding promise of the truth of one's words or that one will do as one says, usually calling upon God as a witness.

offence: an action that breaks the law. **NOTE:** *Offence* is the British spelling of *offense*.

officially: with the authority of the government or some other organization.

oppression: unjust or cruel exercise of authority or power.

ordinance: a rule established by authority; a permanent rule of action.

otherwise: in any other way.

Otis Jr., James: (1725–1783) was an American revolutionary politician from Massachusetts.

ought: used to indicate duty or correctness.

oust: drive out from a position or place; force out.

overarching: encompassing or overshadowing everything.

papers: a document or documents showing somebody's identity or legal status.

paradoxical: if something is paradoxical, it involves two facts or qualities which seem to contradict each other.

paramount: superior to all others; supreme; chief.

parchment: a document or manuscript on paper made from the skin of an animal, usually a sheep or goat, or paper specially treated to resemble this.

Paterson, William: (1745–1806) a New Jersey statesman, a signer of the U.S. Constitution, and Associate Justice of the United States Supreme Court, who served as the 2nd governor of New Jersey, from 1790 to 1793.

peaceably: without war or great disturbance.

penchant: a strong or habitual liking for something or tendency to do something.

penance: the suffering, labor or pain to which a person voluntarily subjects himself, or which is imposed on him by authority as a punishment for his faults.

perjury: the offense of willfully telling an untruth or making a misrepresentation under oath.

persecution: the act of harassing or punishing, especially because of religion, race, or beliefs.

person: the body of a living human being, sometimes including the clothes being worn.

Petition of Right: the Petition of Right is a major English constitutional document, passed by Parliament in 1628, that sets out specific liberties of the subject that the king is prohibited from breaking.

petition: to ask some favor, right, or other benefit from a person or group of persons in authority or power by submitting a formal, written request, often containing the names of people making the request.

pillory: a wooden framework with holes for the head and hands, in which offenders were formerly imprisoned and exposed to public abuse.

Pinckney, Charles: (1757–1824) a U.S. statesman who was a leading member of the convention that framed the U.S. Constitution.

Pitt, William: (1759–1806) a British politician who became the youngest Prime Minister in 1783 at the age of 24 (although the term Prime Minister was not then used).

preamble: an introduction.

precedent: something done or said that may serve as an example to authorize a later act of the same kind; an authoritative example.

precinct: (usually *precincts*) the area within the walls or perceived boundaries of a particular building or place.

prerogative court: 1. in English law, a court where the powers, privileges, and immunities reserved to the sovereign were exercised. In England in the 17th century a clash developed between these courts, representing the crown's authority, and common law courts. **2.** a power, privilege, or immunity restricted to a sovereign or sovereign government.

prescribe: to say with authority that a course of action should be taken; to lay down a rule.

presentment: a report to a court by a Grand Jury, made on its own initiative without a request or presentation of evidence by the local prosecutor, that a "public" crime (illegal act by public officials or affecting the public good) has been committed.

preserve: to defend, maintain or keep unimpaired.

President's Cabinet: a body of advisers to the President, composed of the heads of the executive departments of the government.

pretext: false appearance; apparent reason or motive given or used as a cover for the real reason or motive.

principle: a fundamental idea or belief.

principled: (of a system or method) based on a given set of rules.

Privy Council: in 1540 the Privy Council came into being as a small executive committee appointed by the King or Queen to advise on matters of state and administer the government. Once powerful, the Privy Council has long ceased to be an active body, having lost most of its judicial and political functions since the middle of the 17th century.

probable cause: enough evidence or information to bring a sensible person to believe that an individual is likely to have committed a crime or that evidence of a crime or illegal possessions would be found in a search. Example sentence: The policeman saw a bag of white powder in the trunk and felt it was probable cause to search the car.

probable: likely; having more evidence for it than against it, or evidence that leads you to believe it to be true, but leaves some room for doubt.

prohibit: to stop or get in the way of, prevent or forbid.

pronouncement: a formal or authoritative announcement or declaration.

property: something of value that is owned.

proposition: that which is proposed; that which is offered, as for consideration, acceptance, or adoption; a proposal.

proscribe: to condemn or forbid as harmful or unlawful; prohibit.

prosecution: the pursuit of legal action against someone for compensation for a wrong; the punishment of a crime or the violation of law. Example sentence: The prosecution of the criminal will begin tomorrow.

prostrate: 1. to lay or throw down flat, as on the ground. **2.** to throw one's self down or to fall in humility or worship; to cause to bow in humble reverence.

Protestant: a Christian belonging to one of the three great divisions of Christianity (the other two are the Roman Catholic Church and the Eastern Orthodox Church). Protestantism began during the Renaissance as a protest against the established (Roman Catholic) church. That protest, led by Martin Luther, was called the Reformation, because it sprang from the desire to reform the church and cleanse it of corruption. Protestants hold a great variety of beliefs, but they are united in rejecting the authority of the Pope.

prototype: an original type, form, or instance serving as a basis or standard for later stages.

provide: enable or allow (something to be done).

Providence: God, as the guiding power of the universe.

province: a territory governed as a unit of a country or empire.

provision: a condition or requirement in an agreement, contract, or legal document.

Prynne, William: (1600–1669) an English Puritan leader and pamphleteer. When Prynne's criticism on the theater in his book, *Historiomastix* (1632), was interpreted as an attack on Charles I and his queen, he was pilloried, branded on his forehead, had his ears cut off, was fined heavily, and sentenced to life in prison.

public trial: a trial that is open to and accessible by the public.

public: having to do with a nation, state or community; extending to a whole people, as opposed to private, which indicates what belongs to an individual, group or company.

Pulitzer Prize: a U.S. award for achievements in newspaper and online journalism, literature and musical composition.

Puritanism: a group of radical English Protestants that arose in the late sixteenth century and became a major force in England during the seventeenth century. Puritans wanted to "purify" the Church of England by eliminating traces of its origins in the Roman Catholic Church. In addition, they urged a strict moral code and placed a high value on hard work. After the execution of King Charles I in 1649, they controlled the new government, the Commonwealth. Many Puritans, persecuted in their homeland, came to America in the early 1600s, settling colonies that eventually became Massachusetts.

pursuant to: in agreement with; agreeable; conformable.

quarter: to provide a place to live in for some period of time.

quell: to quiet or calm; to cause to yield or cease.

rack: 1. an instrument of torture having a frame on which the victim's body is bound and stretched until the limbs are pulled out of place. **2.** to torture on a rack.

ratify: to sign or give formal approval of (a treaty, contract, law, or agreement), making it officially valid.

rationale: a set of reasons or a logical basis for a course of action or a particular belief.

reconstitute: to form again or anew; reconstruct, reestablish, or reorganize.

redress: the setting right of what is wrong, often by giving something considered equal to the loss, injury, suffering, lack, etc. Example sentence: The redress of the wrongful punishment included a monetary payment.

regulate: to organize and control an activity or process by rules or laws.

religion: a set of beliefs concerning the cause, nature, and purpose of the universe, especially when considered as the creation of a superhuman entity or entities, usually involving systems of procedures and actions and often containing agreements as to what is right and wrong conduct.

renounce: to refuse to follow, obey, or recognize any further.

repudiate: to refuse to accept; especially to reject as unauthorized or as having no binding force.

repudiation: rejection; the act of refusing to accept or be associated with.

reserve: to keep or hold; to retain.

resolute: having a decided purpose; determined; bold; firm; steady.

resolution: a formal expression of opinion, will, or intent voted by an official body or assembled group.

resolve: to make a decision by a formal vote. Example sentence: The new rules were resolved by the managers.

respecting: regarding; relating to.

respectively: separately and individually and in the order already mentioned.

rest on: be based on or grounded in; depend on.

retain: to keep possession of something.

Revolutionary War: the war for American independence from Britain. The fighting began with the Battles of Lexington and Concord in 1775, and lasted through the Battle of Yorktown in

1781. General George Washington commanded the American forces, assisted by Ethan Allen, Benedict Arnold, Horatio Gates, John Paul Jones, and others. The leaders of the British included Charles Cornwallis, John Burgoyne, Thomas Gage, and William Howe, among others. The American cause was greatly aided by French ships and troops and by the presence of French nobleman and soldier the Marquis de Lafayette. The Treaty of Paris in 1783 officially ended the war.

rhetorical: characterized by the power of persuasion or attraction; that which allures or charms.

right: a legal freedom to have or obtain something or to act in a certain way.

Royal Navy: the British navy.

rule of construction: a phrase used within a legal context to mean "interpretation." The rules are not binding and are better seen as different methods of approaching the interpretation of laws.

said: named or mentioned before.

sanction: to authorize, approve, or allow.

sanguine: bloodthirsty; cruel; eager to shed blood.

scarlet letter: seventeenth century New England punishment for adulteresses requiring they wear a scarlet "A" embroidered on their dress.

schism: a split or division between strongly opposed sections or parties, caused by differences in opinion or belief.

Scripture: also called Holy Scriptures, the sacred writings of the Bible. Often used in the plural.

scrupulous: hesitating to determine or to act; cautious in decision from a fear of offending or doing wrong.

search: to look into, over, or through something carefully in order to find somebody or something.

secure: free from or not exposed to danger, risk, harm or loss; safe.

Sedition Act: an act of Congress passed in 1798 that made it a crime to write anything "false, scandalous or malicious" about the U.S. government or one of its officers; it was used to curb press criticism of government policies.

sedition: conduct or speech enticing people to rebel against the authority of a state or established government.

seditious: inciting or causing people to rebel against the authority of a state or monarch.

seizure: the act of taking something by force or the legal taking of something that belongs to somebody else.

self-incrimination: testimony by a person that reveals facts that may result in a criminal prosecution against him.

Senate: one of the two elected legislative bodies of the United States, composed of 100 members (2 from each state). Representation in the United States Senate is based on the principle of state equality, and the Constitution specifies that no state may be deprived of its equal representation in the Senate without its consent. The Senate is made up of two Senators from each of the fifty states. Most state senates have fewer than fifty members.

Serjeant-at-Law: in England the term applied to the highest class of lawyers.

Sherman, Roger: (1721–1793) an early American lawyer and politician. He served as the first mayor of New Haven, Connecticut, and served on the Committee of Five that drafted the Declaration of Independence. He was the only person to sign all four great state papers of the U.S.: the Continental Association, the Declaration of Independence, the Articles of Confederation, and the Constitution.

shire: in England, a division of territory, otherwise called a county.

sic: used in brackets after a copied or quoted word that appears odd or erroneous to show that the word is quoted exactly as it stands in the original.

society: an organized group of people united either for a temporary or permanent purpose, with laws and traditions that control how they behave toward one another.

sofist: one skilled in elaborate and devious argumentation.

sovereign: 1. possessed of supreme power. 2. the person, body, or state in which independent and supreme authority is vested, especially, in a monarchy, a king, queen, or emperor.

specious: deceptively attractive in appearance.

speech: any declaration of thoughts, whether by words or other means.

standing army: a permanent army of paid soldiers.

standing: settled; established, either by law or by custom; continually existing; permanent; not temporary.

Star Chamber: a royal court existing in England from the 15th century until 1641. The court was set up to ensure the fair enforcement of laws against prominent people, those so powerful that ordinary courts could never convict them of their crimes. Court sessions were held in secret, with no indictments, no right of appeal, no juries, and no witnesses. Evidence was presented in writing. Over time it evolved into a political weapon, a symbol of the misuse and abuse of power by the English monarchy and courts. The name came from the courtroom's ceiling, which was painted with stars.

state: a usually large group of people with their own government, not ruled by any other country; a nation.

statute: a written law passed by a legislative body.

statutory: enacted, created, or regulated by statute, a law passed by a legislative body and set forth in a formal document.

stipend: a fixed regular sum paid as a salary or as expenses to a clergyman, teacher, or public official.

stipulate: 1. demand or specify as part of a bargain or agreement. 2. to make an agreement or contract to do or refrain from doing something.

stoke: add coal or other solid fuel to (a fire, furnace, boiler, etc.); worsen an already bad situation, as by increasing anger, hostility, or passion.

stunt: to hinder the normal growth, development, or progress of.

subject to: to cause to undergo the action of something specified.

subject: one who is under the authority of a ruler and is governed by his laws; one who owes allegiance to a sovereign or a sovereign state.

subjugation: the act, fact, or process of bringing under control; enslavement.

subscribe: to give support or approval; consent or agree (to).

subvert: undermine the power and authority of an established system or institution.

succinct: clearly and briefly stated.

suit: 1. a case brought to a court of law. 2. an action to secure justice in a court of law; an attempt to recover a right or claim through legal action.

summon: to call forth; evoke.

Supreme Court: the highest federal court in the U.S., consisting of nine justices and taking judicial precedence over all other courts in the nation.

systematic: having, showing, or involving a system, method, or plan; purposefully regular.

tacit: not expressed or declared openly, but implied or understood.

Talmudic: having to do with the Talmud, the collection of ancient Jewish writings that forms the basis of Jewish religious law.

tenement: a house; a building for a habitation; or an apartment in a building, used by one family.

thereof: of that or it.

threshold: a strip of wood, metal, or stone forming the bottom of a doorway and crossed in entering a room.

to all intents and purposes: in all important details; in all applications; really.

totalitarian: of, relating to, being, or imposing a form of government in which the political authority exercises absolute and centralized control over all aspects of life, the individual is subordinated to the state, and opposing political and cultural expression is suppressed.

tout: attempt to persuade people of the value or quality of something.

Townshend Acts: a series of laws passed beginning in 1767 by the Parliament of Great Britain relating to the British colonies in North America. The acts are named for Charles Townshend, the Chancellor of the Exchequer, who proposed the program. The laws placed taxes on tea, paper, lead, and paint, imported into the American colonies.

tract: a leaflet or pamphlet containing a declaration or appeal, especially one put out by a religious or political group.

transportation: banishment for crime; deportation.

travesty: a crude, distorted, or ridiculous representation (of something).

treatise: a written composition on a particular subject, in which its principles are discussed or explained.

treaty: a formal agreement or contract between two or more states, such as an alliance or trade arrangement.

trial: a formal examination of the facts and law in a court of law to decide whether someone is innocent or guilty of a crime.

try: to carry out the trial in court of somebody accused of a crime or offense.

two-thirds: two of three equal parts of a whole.

tyranny: cruelty and injustice in the exercising of power or authority over others.

unreasonable: exceeding what is acceptable and in agreement with common sense; claiming or insisting on more than is appropriate.

unto: archaic term for *to*.

usurper: one who takes the place of (someone in a position of power) illegally.

valid: legally effective; having the force of law.

vex: make annoyed or worried.

vilify: to make hurtful and abusive statements about somebody.

violate: to break or ignore a law, agreement, etc.

Virginia Declaration of Rights: a document drafted in 1776 to proclaim the inherent rights of men, including the right to rebel against "inadequate" government. It influenced a number of later documents, including the United States Declaration of Independence and the United States Bill of Rights.

viz: that is to say (used especially to introduce examples, details, etc.). **NOTE:** *Viz* is an abbreviation of the Latin word *videlicet*, which means *that is; namely*.

wantonly: (of a cruel or violent action) deliberately and unprovoked.

Ward, Nathaniel: (1578–1652) a Puritan, clergyman, and pamphleteer in England and Massachusetts. He wrote the first constitution in North America in 1641.

warrant: a legal document issued by an authority that allows someone to legally do something which he would normally not have the right to do, such as search another's car or arrest another.

West Indies: a string of islands in the North Atlantic between North and South America, comprising the Greater Antilles, the Lesser Antilles, and the Bahamas.

wheel: a medieval torture consisting of a wheel to which the victim was tied and then had his limbs hit and broken by an iron bar.

wherein: in which place. Example sentence: This is the arena wherein the Super Bowl was held.

Whig: a member of a major political party (1679–1832) in Great Britain that held liberal principles and favored reforms; later called the Liberal party.

Wilkes, John: (1725–1797) an English radical, journalist, and politician.

Wilson, James: (1742–1798) one of the Founding Fathers of the United States and a signer of the United States Declaration of Independence. Wilson was elected twice to the Continental Congress, and was a major force in drafting the United States Constitution. Wilson was one of the six original justices appointed by George Washington to the Supreme Court of the United States.

witness: a person who gives a statement under oath or affirmation, usually in a court of law.

writ of assistance: a written order (a writ) issued by a court instructing a law enforcement official, such as a sheriff, to perform a certain task. In United States colonial history, writs of assistance were issued to help customs officials search for smuggled goods.

writ: a form of written command in the name of a court or other legal authority to act, or refrain from acting, in some way.

Also by Sean Patrick

Awakening Your Inner Genius

If you'd like to know what some of history's greatest thinkers and achievers can teach you about awakening your inner genius, and how to find, follow, and fulfill your journey to greatness, then you want to read this book today.

Visit www.yourinnergenius.com to learn more about this book!

Made in United States
Troutdale, OR
09/12/2024

22758510R00139